Dani
THROWAWAY CHILD

Dani: Throwaway Child

Second Edition

Copyright © 2017 B D Ethington. All Rights Reserved.

No rights claimed for public domain material, all rights reserved. No parts of this publication may be reproduced, stored in any retrieval system, or transmitted in any form or by any means, electronic, mechanical, recording, or otherwise, without the prior written permission of the author. Violations may be subject to civil or criminal penalties.

Library of Congress Control Number: 2017947784

ISBN: 978-1-63308-275-5 (paperback)
       978-1-63308-276-2 (ebook)

Cover and Interior Design by *R'tor John D. Maghuyop*

1028 S Bishop Avenue, Dept. 178
Rolla, MO 65401

Printed in United States of America

Dani
THROWAWAY CHILD

*The True Story of Dani's Journey
from Abuse to Freedom*

SECOND EDITION

B D Ethington

CHALFANT ECKERT
PUBLISHING

DEDICATION

This book is dedicated to Dani
and her family for their courage, bravery, and faith.
It is also dedicated to Dani's support network of friends
who reached out to help her end her nightmare and have
a normal, happy life. My brother and his wife played a vital role
in this story and a simple thank you is not enough.
I also dedicate this book to all those who live with
or have endured the horrors of abuse similar
to what Dani experienced.

TABLE OF CONTENTS

A Brief Word about Confidential Interviews 7
Prologue 9

Chapter 1   *I Meet Dani for the First Time* 13
Chapter 2   *Dani Begins to Communicate* 27
Chapter 3   *Finding Clarity Amid Chaos* 33
Chapter 4   *Power and Control* 39
Chapter 5   *A New Dani Begins to Emerge* 49
Chapter 6   *Please Make Them Stop* 55
Chapter 7   *The Flood Gates Open* 61
Chapter 8   *A Normal Beginning* 69
Chapter 9   *Life Gets Worse* 81
Chapter 10   *Life in a Closet* 93
Chapter 11   *Throwaway Child* 105
Chapter 12   *The Rules* 119
Chapter 13   *New Rules* 135
Chapter 14   *God, Where Are You?* 149
Chapter 15   *An Unexpected Revelation* 161
Chapter 16   *Why Can't They Stop?* 173
Chapter 17   *Clouds of Darkness Gather* 185
Chapter 18   *Escaping Abuse* 195
Chapter 19   *Happily Ever After?* 207

Epilogue 211
Resources 217
References 219

A BRIEF WORD ABOUT CONFIDENTIAL INTERVIEWS

You are about to read a true story from a religious leader's perspective. Dani's story is the culmination of confidential interviews of actual memories and experiences over time. Interviews between faith leaders and their parishioners are based on trust and held in the strictest confidence. This trust is not taken lightly and was NEVER broken. Dani has given her written permission to utilize these interviews to tell her story. Her true identity remains confidential to protect her and her family. All the names were changed for their safety.

At first, Dani hesitated to tell her story, mainly for her safety and that of her children. She eventually concluded that if her story could give courage and hope to the abused as well as insight to those helping them, it would be worth sharing. Dani was courageous to come forth and even more courageous to allow me to tell her story. We hope that her courage will become infectious in helping the thousands of women and children who still live with abuse every day. Our hearts and prayers go out to those individuals.

President John F. Kennedy credited the 1770s Irish statesman and philosopher Edmund Burke as having said, "All that is necessary for the triumph of evil is that good men do nothing" (in *Documents on Disarmament 1961*, 1962). This statement is so true. If we fail to act, to come to someone's rescue, whether out of fear of not wanting to get involved or feeling that it is none of our business, then we may be responsible to God for those we could have saved. It doesn't take a faith leader to take action. It takes all of us who are or call ourselves followers of Christ to observe, act, and do. This book could be your call to action in the hidden war of abuse that is raging against our women and children. May we adopt the words of the great hymn, "Fear not, though the enemy deride, Courage, For the Lord is on Our Side" (Stephens, 1977).

This story is from the perspective of a Bishop in The Church of Jesus Christ of Latter-day Saints, also known as the Mormon Church. A Bishop is the head of a congregation of members and is called to serve

A Brief Word about Confidential Interviews

as a lay clergy in this capacity. In other words, all members who serve in the church do so without monetary compensation. Congregations are typically comprised of members who live within a geographic area called a *ward*. Bishops are ordained to lead, serve, and care for the members living within the boundaries of their ward. Members promise to live by a Christ-like code of morality.

PROLOGUE

The Mirror

Time. It has a way of losing its intrinsic value when there is nothing to compare its passing. The rising and lowering of the sun, the movements of a clock or even the routine and habitual movements of people waking in the morning, going to bed at night. All these can give one the value of time to denote days, months, or even years passing. But to someone kept in a dark closet with little or no light and even less of human contact, time has no beginning or end. It just is.

For Dani, it could have been days that she had sat there in the closet tucked away in a bedroom of the house. All she could see was some light filtering through cracks in the door frame or under the door. The daylight gave her some delineation of passing days, but she had little to give her any indication of how long she had been in there or when it might end. What little light filtered through into the closet was just enough for Dani to see some of her surroundings. The closet had a hardwood floor with smooth plaster walls surrounding an area with just enough space to sit and stretch but not to walk around. It was completely vacant except for her. The bar that stretched the length of the enclosure was bare. Such pretty dresses used to hang there, she remembered.

Dani was dressed only in her underwear. She typically sat in one corner with her knees drawn up to her chest encircled by her arms. When that position became uncomfortable, she would shift from one side to the other or lay down to sleep. By now she had gotten used to having the hardwood floor double as her bed. The soft covers and fluffy pillow on the bed she once used were now but a longing even though they were only a few feet away. Sleeping on the bed was forbidden, and she dared not even try. They would find out, they always did.

One day her mother had systematically removed everything Dani had come to know was hers. At first, her mother took her eyeglasses, then her shoes. Toys and books were followed by her clothes first landing in the

PROLOGUE

hallway, then swept away to some unknown place. All her possessions had been taken away, except for one which she kept hidden in the closet.

She didn't know how long it had been, but she remembered seeing a shadow cross in front of the door. Someone was in the bedroom. She tensed, anticipating a beating or worse, but nothing happened. Then the shadow crossed again in front of the door. Involuntarily, she hugged her legs tighter and backed as far as she could into the corner of the small room. When the door did not open, she began to relax a bit.

It had been a long time since she had eaten. Worse than the gnawing hunger in her stomach was the empty feeling of loneliness. Since being in her new room, she had not seen any member of the family. Even poor treatment would be preferable to no contact at all. Sometimes she wept but was careful to do it silently so as not to attract attention and then certain punishment.

A shadow crossed the front of the door again. This time, she was more curious than afraid. Who could it be? What were they doing? Somebody paused outside the door. She strained her ears to hear who the mystery person might be on the other side. A faint scratching noise near the bottom of the door caught her attention.

Dani watched an object slowly pushed under the door. Fearing a trick or a deception she didn't reach for it at first. The shadow retreated away, and Dani sat staring at it for several minutes. Slowly she reached out and touched the object then quickly pulled her hand back. After repeating the process a couple more times and realizing that it was no threat, she finally picked up the object. In the dim light, she ran her finger over the edge of the object. The top part was circular, approximately four inches in diameter with a handle extending from the rounded edge. She explored the object by turning it over and around until she saw a reflection which startled her so much she almost dropped the object. Her heart skipped a beat. It was a mirror!

Smiling, she hugged the object. For the first time in as long as she could remember, she felt happy inside. What a treasure she now possessed. With all the care of an archeologist handling rare antiquities, she carefully slid the object in a notch in the corner of the closet which would keep it hidden from the casual observer. Her new prize now safely hidden, she pulled her legs up and wrapped her arms around them to generate some warmth. After a while, she closed her eyes and fell asleep with a small smile resting on her lips.

"I need you to do something for me," Dani said with somewhat pleading eyes. I could see she had thought a lot about this and had finally reached a point where she felt that I could be trusted.

"What would you like me to do?" I asked.

She hesitated, not speaking a single word. She gazed off into the distance for a time. She seemed to be seeing something beyond the plainly decorated walls of my office.

We had been talking for over a half an hour. She had been telling me about some of her weekly struggles. Kids with colds that never seemed to go away, husband working long hours, and that she wasn't getting much sleep. Her report was now interrupted by her request.

With great care, she reached into her bag and pulled out an object wrapped in tissue paper. Careful removal of the covering revealed that the object was a small mirror. It was approximately four inches in diameter encased in purple plastic with a handle extending from it. It was obvious that the mirror was aged, and it looked more like a toy. She carefully handed it to me.

"I want you to keep this for me," she requested.

Even though it looked like a toy, she handled it with reverence and care, her expression revealing it to be like a cherished old friend. As she gently handed it to me, I became aware that it meant a lot to her, and she was trusting this special treasure into my care. Even without carefully observing the object I knew that there was a story behind the worn plastic edges and the carefully polished glass of the mirror.

CHAPTER 1

I Meet Dani for the First Time

"In the middle of difficulty lies opportunity."
—Albert Einstein

The confines of her space were dark and oppressive. Why was it so dark? Stuffy and claustrophobic, she could hardly breathe. It was frightening and yet simultaneously comforting. Oddly she felt that she was somehow safe. Oh yes, the closet, her safe place. Fear. Was that what she was feeling? That was what it was, fear! Steps were coming, loud voices, yelling! Why were they yelling? She knew that it was about something she did, but what? It was always about something she did. She searched her memory but could find nothing. If she could just understand what she had done, maybe she could make it all better; make it all stop! Why couldn't she remember?

The yelling stopped! Footsteps came closer and closer. Fear again! Why? She just couldn't remember. Why couldn't she remember? She suddenly felt panic. The door to the closet opened. Somehow, she knew what was going to happen. A face without features, angry and mean, obscured by the darkness, was yelling words and obscenities. They were hurtful, painful words. Why? She didn't understand. Then there was another faceless head. So close. Yelling and screaming. Then out of the darkness something was coming at her. She sensed it coming but it was too late to protect herself. It hit with vicious force. The pain! Oh, the awful pain! Then it came again and again and again! "Stop!" she yelled. "Please stop! Please!" She sobbed. "Please!" Her response was just a whimper now, almost without hope.

Mercifully there was some light. She knew she had to reach the light. "Focus," she thought. "Just focus and you can do it." She mustered the last bit of strength she had and reached out through the pain to the light. Slowly the voices began to fade as the light got stronger. She struggled to open her eyes. As she did so, the faces also seemed to melt away and the closet evaporated as if in wisps of smoke. She panicked! What was she going to do without her safe haven?

As she opened her eyes she realized she had been screaming. She was gasping great gulps of air as if she had been drowning and now found herself above water. The words still seemed to echo in her ears. She didn't have to look; she knew she was covered in sweat. As the panic subsided and her breathing calmed, she realized once again where she was. She was home. She was in her own home! She could see the night light on the wall just a few feet from her. It had saved her again.

Another nightmare! This realization set in as she more fully awakened. Why didn't they stop? What were they about? All she knew is that when she woke up, she was exhausted, dripping in sweat, and she felt like she had just been savagely beaten. She realized that she was in another safe place; the same place she ended up after each of these nightmares. She was under her bed. The reality of finding herself huddled in the cramped space below the comfort of her mattress was extremely troubling to her, but the familiar place was mysteriously comforting.

The sun peered through the bedroom window ushering in a new day. From her place under the bed she could see its welcoming light streak across the floor. Despite the fatigue generated by lack of sleep, she needed to get up and take care of her children. She knew the memory of the nightmare would fade if she just busied herself getting the kids off to school and began her daily routine of housework. The pain, however, would remain. Not the emotional pain from hurtful words and angry shouts, but deep physical pain that accompanied each dream. She knew she would feel that pain most of the day.

She also knew something else . . . she needed help! She couldn't keep going on like this.

Sometimes our lives seem to be filled with meetings. For some, these events can be welcome diversions from a mundane daily routine and others a chance to be a part of meaningful discussions. Still others, like me, can find meetings to be a frustrating bridge between the items that *must* be done on a daily To-Do list. I was definitely in this last category. Pretending to listen, I was both distracted and slightly bored.

The meeting in which I was seated was very important to the organizer, however, I was not feeling its relevancy. The attendees in the room were all faith leaders from the various churches in our local area. As I looked around, I realized that only a few seemed to share my detached perspective and I felt slightly embarrassed.

I certainly was not focused on the speaker. He was stressing how child abuse was a real problem in our community. Statistics of reported abuse and reported hospital visits were only a drop in the bucket to the amount of abuse that, sadly, goes unreported. Like all of us in attendance, we found abuse, especially that of a child, to be repugnant and loathsome.

Regretfully my attention was elsewhere, but it seemed to be completely justified. Most of my congregation was young families. Weekly I was meeting with and getting to know many of them quite well. Even knowing many of the problems challenging some of these families, I could not imagine that any of them could be involved with abuse. The topic just wasn't relevant to me at the moment and I did not anticipate that I would ever need any of this information.

As the speakers presented their information I sat politely taking occasional notes. When the meeting ended, I gathered the information and prepared statistics and guidelines, then made a bee-line towards the door to take care of my 'must' items. When I got home, I filed the papers away without any notion of ever using them.

If I had only foreseen the events that would start to unfold, I would not have been so casual about the meeting or the information. Hence the saying: *Live and learn.*

I am not only a bishop with a congregation but I am also a father with children. The angelic nature of children is a gift to any parent. Children are so eager to love and be loved. They naturally desire to explore the world around them. When they see a butterfly for the first time or catch a falling snow flake, most parents' hearts swell with appreciation for their little ones' purity and innocence.

Parents are also innately fierce protectors. My own fatherly experience has more than once found me feeling personally violated when one of my own children was threatened, endangered, or confronted by bullies. Like Christ in the Holy Temple, I have felt like braiding a cord and thrashing the violators. I think that most parents feel the same way. This natural protective disposition arises whenever I see or hear an adult threatening and abusing a child. I have wished on more than one occasion to have the power and courage to fiercely face such abusers, and with a voice of thunder let them know how divinely special children are to God. I would follow my tirade with a look that clearly communicated to them that if they laid a hand on their children, a raw steak would be placed around their neck and they would be set in the middle of a pack of wolves. I don't as a rule carry raw steak with me and have no idea how to find a hungry wolf much less a pack of them, but they certainly would feel the power of my message.

I guess that is why I felt so compelled to tell this story about Dani. Most of what happened to her occurred while she was a small child. Those who should have been responsible to care for her and give her both love and protection, did just the opposite. Despite all that has happened to her, she has survived and is amazingly normal, whatever 'normal' means. I have never written a book before, but my experience with Dani has been the catalyst to my first literary try. There has been a nagging prompting deep inside, pushing me to make sure that her story is told. My hope is that it will be an inspiration to other innocent victims who have themselves been in similar situations and to all feeling people wanting to make a difference for the abused.

The first time I met Dani was under some slightly unusual circumstances. Her Bishop had called me to tell me she and her family had moved into my church ward and that he would like to introduce me to the family so that there was some continuity. I thought that 'continuity' was an interesting word. Continuity about what, I wondered. I set a date and time to meet with him at his office.

A call like this was kind of unusual, not because she was moving near our church ward, but because most people move in and then just start attending. We had well over 300 additional people move into our ward family during the previous year. Low interest rates and increasing demand for home building had caused explosive growth in our area, which seemed to be a magnet attracting young families. Like magic, new homes were popping up almost overnight. Families were moving in as fast as developers finished construction. Families belonging to our faith just showed up and were never introduced by their former bishop. Without explanation, there was obviously something unique about this communication from her previous bishop.

The following Sunday I arrived early at the other bishop's office. As I entered I noticed the large, framed, reproduction paintings of Jesus Christ as well as some of His apostles on the walls. I also noticed comfortable cushioned chairs positioned around the room focused toward a single desk at one end of the room. It appeared to be a typical bishop's office, simple and yet comfortable. As he introduced himself, I observed he was tall, well dressed, and looked smart in a pinstripe suit. I was also amazed how young he was. He couldn't have been more than in his late twenties. He greeted me warmly and turned to the young family waiting to meet me.

Seated in the cushioned seats was a broad-shouldered man, his petite wife, and their three children seated strategically between them. I shook hands with the young man and learned his name was Jeff. He was a construction worker with a strong grip and a winning smile. His calloused hands echoed that his work involved manual labor. He was about my height and slightly thinner. His appearance was rough, yet he displayed a genuine, sensitive side made evident when I saw him glance lovingly at his wife. Two of the children, in true childlike fashion dangled their legs off the edge of their chairs. The oldest was Cami who was ten years old, tall and thin like her father and she had a piercing stare. Jenny was eight, precocious, overly friendly and seemed to enjoy laughing even when there was nothing to laugh at. The youngest, Jake, was playing a game of hide-and-seek with me, peeking from behind his blanket in the car seat. He was about six months old and cute as a button. From initial appearances, they looked to be the typical, average American family.

Lastly, I was introduced to Dani. She was not at all what I had expected. She was only slightly taller than her oldest daughter at about five feet tall. Her eyes were a vivid green and her natural blonde hair might have looked lovely had she had not pulled it unceremoniously back into a ponytail. Her hair did not have that cared-for touch and her clothes hung loosely on her, not because they were too big, but because she was so thin. Even covered with clothes I could see that her arms and legs were mostly skin and bones. I could not help but thinking that she must be anorexic.

She quickly caught my gaze and I noticed a brief look of surprise. She averted her eyes instantly, obviously feeling uncomfortable with the attention drawn to her. I couldn't tell if she was naturally shy or if she was just very private. The brief glance revealed a sadness in her eyes. The thought occurred to me that she hadn't smiled in a long, long time. When I offered my hand she rapidly looked up but did not respond in kind. There was what appeared to be a brief look of recognition on her face. I was quite puzzled by the experience and subsequently was left wondering what it was all about. I was certain I had never seen her before in my life.

"Thank you for coming. This is the family I called you about." I knew that this Bishop was a lay minister like myself. We were both called to watch over our flocks.

After brief introductions, he continued. "This is the Moss family. They have recently built a home in your area and will be attending church with your congregation. They have been hesitant to attend so far because they don't know anyone. I thought by having you come today they would at least know you." He smiled weakly at the attempt to bring me into the conversation.

I returned the smile and assured them that we were more than happy to have them be a part of our growing congregation. I explained that we had an excellent program for the children, and that with so many new young families arriving in the past year that they would fit right in. I also told them that we met at 9:00 a.m. each Sunday morning. Jeff paid close attention to the information, it looked as though he was the only one who noticed.

"I have been meeting with Dani about once a week for the last month or two," he continued. "She seems to do better if we meet weekly. I was hoping that you could continue the weekly sessions. Would that be okay?"

"That would be just fine." I replied as I was mentally determining appointment openings. "And can you give me some idea why we are meeting?" I looked at Dani. She was not looking at me. The pattern on her handbag seemed to be occupying all her attention.

"She just has some personal things she wants to discuss. That's all," her bishop replied as he observed Dani and her unresponsive manner.

"Very well, then," I said turning to Dani, "Would Sunday at 4:00 o'clock in the afternoon be okay for our first meeting?" She looked up briefly and nodded in agreement and then continued staring down.

Sensing that the brief meeting was over, I stood and said goodbye to the Moss family as I watched them exit the room. As I headed toward the door, her bishop asked if I could remain for a minute longer. He closed the door and sat back down.

"I didn't want to say much. Dani is struggling with something serious. She has an eating disorder as you can probably tell. As hard as I have tried, I have not been able to get her to discuss much with me. Jeff doesn't seem to have a clue. I just know something is wrong."

"What type of counseling have you been doing?" I asked even though I knew that due to confidentiality he would not be able tell me a great deal, if anything at all. I was not surprised with his answer.

"Not much. I mostly just sit and listen." He had a faraway look in his eye. "I mostly just sit and listen. But if we don't meet every week she is visibly shaken, it is like she needs the interview to stay grounded or something."

Listening shouldn't be too hard, I thought. I am a good listener. I said goodbye and left pondering about my brief visit with the Moss family and wondering about that first appointment on Sunday with Dani.

Our first meeting was pretty uneventful. Dani came in and sat across the desk from me. She said very little. Her blonde hair was still pulled back in a ponytail. She also wore a long sleeve shirt much too large for her small frame. Perhaps it belonged to her husband. She was nearly swallowed up in the extra fabric.

I asked her about her family and what she liked to do for fun. She didn't offer too much, although talking about her family was most likely less intimidating than talking about what the real issues were that bothered her.

One thing I found strange was that she kept glancing at the door each time there was a pause in the conversation. It was as if she was expecting something to happen with that door. I concluded that she was in an obviously uncomfortable setting and she could hardly wait to leave. Maybe something about me was scaring her. Indications were that our first interview was not going so well. I kept plowing ahead in spite of the awkwardness in the primarily one-sided conversation.

On the surface, she appeared to be quite average. Several months after meeting Jeff, they fell in love, got married, and started having children. There were certain things I would ask that she would avoid and others she was excited to talk about. Dani especially loved to talk about her children and it was obvious that she was very proud of them. Her face beamed as she described how her children were full of energy and fun. Cami and Jenny loved school and were getting good grades. Dani enjoyed driving them to school and picking them up, taking them to swim lessons as well as to the store. Overall, she appeared to be a normal young mother with a typical family.

I didn't really expect that she would instantly open up to me and share her deepest and darkest secrets. These things take time and trust. Whatever she was struggling with did not seem to be within her family. She genuinely loved her husband and adored her children. I was perplexed at what could be causing her eating disorder.

While we talked she continued to keep looking at the door. The anticipated knock or interruption never came. When she left, she lowered her eyes and said, "Thank you." Was she just shy or embarrassed or scared? I pondered these things as she drove off. What was looking repeatedly at the door all about? Was she afraid that she could be overheard or maybe that someone might find out that she was there? At that point, there were more questions than answers. I realized that I understood less about this petite young woman after this first meeting than I had anticipated. One thing I felt certain of: She was afraid of something or someone. Unable to determine if I had helped her or not, I felt assured that at the next appointment maybe we would make more progress.

As I approached my office door I found my next appointment waiting for me. We shook hands as I closed the door. I had two more appointments before I would be able to go home and eat dinner with my family.

During the next several visits Dani became more vocal, so I just let her talk while I simply listened. I didn't take any notes because I felt that could be a distraction, making her feel uncomfortable. She was going to need to feel comfortable and secure before we could establish an honest dialogue. I hoped she could become confident enough in me to open up. During lulls in the conversation when she seemed to have reached the end of her thoughts, I would ask questions. She responded to those about her family. I started to learn which questions to avoid and which ones revealed her comfort zone.

She continued to glance at the door off and on during the hour interview. She didn't seem anxious to leave. Our session was uninterrupted just like our first one. This left me wondering why the door held her attention so often during our time together.

Like an early morning fog slowly lifting, Dani was slowly letting go of her mistrust and gaining confidence in sharing more of her personal life with me. She would occasionally test me to see how I would react. If I handled it to her satisfaction she would trust me with a few more tidbits. It almost felt like I was, perhaps, cracking a safe open by allowing the tumblers to fall into place one at a time. If I asked the right questions and responded appropriately, then another tumbler would fall into place. Eventually I hoped to find the right combination that would allow me to help her through whatever struggle she was going through.

At the end of one interview she caught me off guard. With a look of alarm, she said, "Is it safe here?" Her face looked gripped with fright.

"What do you mean *safe*?" I asked.

"Safe!" she almost demanded with a touch of panic in her voice. "You know, safe!"

Was that why she was looking at the door all the time? Was she worried about it being safe? But from what or better yet, whom?

"Do you mean is it safe talking to me? Yes!" I assured her. "This room is safe, Dani. Whatever you tell me in this room stays in this room unless you give me permission to tell someone. Otherwise, it stays right here. So, yes, it is safe!" I was going to describe the additional soundproofing in the walls, the solid oak door and the white noise projector just outside the door, but the spirit impressed me that that wasn't going to be necessary.

She seemed to relax a little bit. "Are you sure?"

"I am sure!" I said confidently.

"Okay." She then visibly relaxed.

We continued our conversation as though it had never occurred. This process repeated itself each session for the next several weeks almost word for word. She would think about it, almost processing the words, and then relax each time. She was genuinely worried or scared about something. I was unsure as to whether I should be concerned or not. In spite of her concerns for safety, I really felt like we were making progress. She seemed to be more relaxed although she would sit in her chair, pull her knees to her chest, and wrap her arms tightly around them. It was a protective gesture for sure.

These first several weeks were a testing period for the both of us. I was testing her to see what subjects we could cover and what she would allow me to discover. She was testing me to see if she could trust me and if I had a genuine desire to help her. During one of our early sessions she told me that she knew who I was during that very first meeting.

"When I saw you for the first time, I was kinda scared. I knew you the moment I saw you."

"I don't remember meeting or seeing you before. How is that possible?" I asked.

She told me simply and innocently that during one of her moments of despair she prayed to God for help.

"I was almost about to take my life. I just couldn't handle anymore. While I was praying, I don't know if I was dreaming or not, I saw an angel." She paused to see if I was going to believe her. I knew that this was another test. I didn't respond but listened intently.

"The angel," she continued, "told me to be patient and wait. Help was on the way. The angel told me that God was preparing someone that would help me." At this point she paused. With a rare show of emotion, she wiped a tear from her eye before continuing.

"It was in that moment that I saw you, sitting here in your office at this desk and wearing this same suit. The angel assured me that you could help me. I knew when you came into my life that I needed you because God sent you to help me. It just took me a while to finally trust you," she said.

That conversation remains powerfully with me as if it happened yesterday. In addition to the words she spoke, I also remember the electrical shock that went through me at that moment. Here was a divine witness that she had moved into my ward by heavenly guidance and God had prepared and called me to be there to help her at this precise moment. This was one of many miracles that we would experience over the following months.

There were signs that she was starting to feel safe. She still wouldn't make eye contact all the time, but she started opening up about more areas of her life. I learned that she was seeing a psychiatrist. This doctor was helping Dani express herself through pictures and drawings. She indicated that she found she could tell her story in pictures. She could express herself this way because her story was too difficult to talk about. Her psychiatrist was also helping her with some other issues she was not willing to discuss at this point. So, I was patient and had a reassuring feeling that when the time was right she would feel comfortable in sharing with me what was bothering her.

When she began to feel somewhat at ease we discussed the first visible issue: an eating disorder. She would eat and later throw up. She was very self-conscious about her weight. She saw herself as fat and excessively overweight. Due to the relative immediate dangers of this behavior, I felt it needed immediate corrective action. From my point of view, her vision of her body seemed absurd. She was slim, tiny, and petite. Her fingers and hands were boney. She was careful to keep her arms and legs covered. I could only imagine they were in the same condition. I came to understand that when she looked in the mirror she saw herself as overweight, fat, undesirable, and imperfect.

As our interview continued we were able to discuss a more unsettling issue that she had -a compulsive addiction known as *cutting*. She would regularly take a razor blade and cut parts of her body. Some would be deep cuts that required lots of time to heal and recover. When I asked her if this hurt when she did it, she let me know that she did it for the pain. She liked the pain. My imagination tried to understand how painful this must be to her.

Googling an article on WebMD.com, I learned the following: "Cutting is a form of self-injury - the person is literally making small cuts on his or her body, usually the arms and legs. It's difficult for many people to understand. But for kids, cutting helps them control their emotional pain, psychologists say" (David, n.d.). The insight that the pain of cutting was masking some real pain that she was feeling was significant.

Both issues, cutting and liking the pain it created, seriously weighed on my mind and I was at a loss of how to begin helping her. There was some comfort knowing that Dani was receiving professional help. I decided that since I was not trained in these areas that leaving these disorders to the professionals was the best approach. I also concluded that these issues were most likely an exterior manifestation of other deeper issues that she was not willing to talk about yet.

Dani also commented on how tired and lethargic she was. Her mind seemed to be clouded and she couldn't remember things. As we talked I learned that she was on medication, not just one medication but many prescriptions at the same time. As long as she could remember, medications had been a daily regimen for her. When I asked her what the medications were for, she said she didn't know. All she knew is that she was told that she needed them. She indicated that there were some medications that the doctor had prescribed for her and then some that her dad had insisted she had to take.

I knew just enough about medications to know that they can exhibit both good and bad effects. A medication can eliminate the main symptom and yet cause other, sometimes unrelated side effects. Multiple medications taken at the same time, if not properly monitored, could create extreme reactions and unusual behaviors. I knew I had to keep that in mind as I helped Dani.

It seemed like Dani had many challenges which stacked the odds against her for a normal life. I knew I could help her spiritually which would give her hope and strength. This would be a foundation for her to handle all the challenges in her life. We were still building a bond of complete trust. This was essential before I could help Dani achieve any true progress and overcome these challenges and any others that may be lying in wait. She needed God's strength in her life as well as someone she could trust and rely on to help her. Never before had I felt the weight of such an undertaking. As I left my office for the night, I resolved that I wouldn't worry about things that were best left to professionals. I felt determined to help her find strength in an all-loving God. Time and time again, He had been there for me and I knew that He would be there for her as well.

CHAPTER 2

Dani Begins to Communicate

"Hope is a waking dream."
−Aristotle

The enclosure was dark and cold. These conditions didn't bother her as much as being alone. She ached for her mother. Where was she? Why didn't she come when she called out to her? Feeling around to determine where she was, her hands came in contact with the unfinished room. The cold concrete floor and the rough wooden vertical beams with sheet rock on the other side. The thin walls usually allowed sounds filtering down the stairs to the basement as the family talked, sang, or played but she had heard nothing for hours. Anxiously she called again to her mother but heard no response.

For several minutes, she sobbed not knowing or understanding where she was or why. She felt totally alone. Fear welled up inside her as she tried to understand her predicament. How had she gotten here? Where was her family? Then she realized why she was so cold. She was only wearing her underwear and she was standing on a concrete floor. An uncontrollable shiver went through her. Instinctively she sought for a place of comfort and warmth, neither of which could be found in the small confines of the closet.

Finally, she stopped crying and reached for the door knob. As she did so, fear gripped her. Why? She didn't know. Each time she reached for it she felt as though something awful was going to happen. Loneliness and shivering overcame the fear she was experiencing and she slowly turned the door knob. The door slowly opened on creaking hinges revealing an outer room with no light. Slowly, cautiously, she stepped forward into the dark. She froze in mid-step. Instinctively she knew the blow was coming before it landed. She started to cry as she received blow after blow.

"Where are you going, you worthless piece of garbage?"

Once more fear overwhelmed her as she felt the first blow, and then another and another. She started to cry. The hitting stopped briefly.

"Stop that! Do you hear? You know it will be worse if you make any noise," the harsh voice spat the command in a hushed tone.

Tears ran down her cheeks as she felt the blows land. She dared not make any noise except a small whimpering sound when the pain was too much. Then, mercifully, her knees buckled and darkness overcame her. Slowly she processed a waking sensation, her mind feeling enveloped in a black sea that was filled with loneliness and pain. She found herself gaining consciousness, to discover once again being under her bed, pushed up far against the wall. This time she did not worry about making any noise. Burying her head in her hands, she sobbed and sobbed.

It was a great relief knowing that there were professionals helping Dani; counselors who were trained to help with severe disorders and emotional struggles. I was sure that these professionals would skillfully unravel whatever events had caused the disorders and resolve the pain they caused.

I felt that listening was my best approach. She was responding well as I made little comments and asked questions during our interviews. This seemed to help her talk about anything she wanted to discuss. Until now I avoided any topic I had found that caused her to withdraw and refuse to talk.

Slowly she was starting to emerge into another Dani. It was as if she was becoming two different people. During most of our discussions, a more confident and determined young woman started to blossom.

Then, without warning, she would revert back into her old self: quiet, drooping posture, downcast eyes, and visibly scared. She would pull her legs up to the seat of the chair and wrap her arms around them. She would even withdraw and become nearly unresponsive to my questions.

Her personality evidently would change accordingly to topics we discussed. When we talked about things that centered on her family or her children's school activities, her personality would transform into a confident young woman chattering freely about family life, her children, yard work, car problems, etc. Having no professional counseling experience, this behavior was puzzling and I didn't know what any of it meant, but still there was a feeling that we were making some real progress. Progress to where, I didn't know, but those little positive moves forward felt wonderful. Certainly, any progress had to be good.

Dani also shared with me that she had told her psychiatrist about our interviews. The doctor had told Dani that I was really helping her. With only the Spirit as my guide, I literally had no idea of what I was doing that was helping, yet the doctor's stated confidence in me increased her confidence in me as well.

As Dani became more comfortable with our conversations, she learned that she did not have to hide her responses. She also showed a natural innocence that at times was both naive and devoid of any pretense. I got the distinct impression that her emotions had been suppressed to the point that she couldn't or wouldn't express any type of response. Had Dani been scolded or criticized so that she was afraid to respond? Was she fearful that my response might be critical? My hope that as she became more confident in our relationship she would communicate what was so troubling.

One Sunday afternoon, quite out of the blue, Dani asked me if she could show me something. She explained that her doctor was having her put together collages with the intent of helping her communicate her ideas, feelings, and thoughts that she just couldn't verbalize.

"I would love to see them," I responded with enthusiasm, "as long as it is alright with you."

She seemed rather pleased and then glanced at the door. "Is it safe?" she asked.

I almost laughed, but didn't. "Yes, it is safe!" She seemed more concerned than usual. It was as though she was going to tell some secret and didn't want anyone to hear. She expressed a much more serious plea when she asked the question a second time.

"Is it SAFE?"

"Yes," I replied emphatically, "it is safe."

Dani smiled and visibly relaxed. She reached for a red folder she had placed on the floor by her chair and pulled out a stiff sheet of paper which was slightly larger than a regular sheet of paper. As I looked at it I was startled. I consciously had to hide my gut reaction from my facial expression. This was very important to her and she needed me to remain objective.

The picture was an intricate collection of snippets and cutouts from magazines and newspapers. Large and small pieces were blended together mixing colors and images into an intricate story. I had to study it for quite a while. My first impression was that it was dark and foreboding. Then, as I studied it further, I could see images of a woman or girl in the shadows, barely visible, almost hidden. I could see words like *hurt, broken trust, painful, broken heart,* and *why?* Each set of words was cut out in tiny strips and pasted at various angles next to or on top of other shadowy figures looking like women or young girls. It appeared as though the images of the half-hidden women wanted to tell their secret but were unable to do so. Hidden in the intricate pictures of the collage were eyes that had been blacked out as though what they had witnessed was unspeakable. I had never seen anything quite like it before.

"Well, what do you think?" she asked expectantly.

"It is really quite beautiful," I replied, feeling at a loss for appropriate words.

She crinkled her nose. "It's not beautiful," she said, chiding me.

I had failed to elicit the correct response. Was Dani expecting me to be able to instantly understand the story she was trying to tell?

"Let's put it this way," I said trying another approach, "it is rather amazing. It looks as though you must have spent hours on this to find all the right pictures and phrases to use. It is quite well done. You are very talented."

Now she smiled with a touch of embarrassment at the complement but she didn't allow it to last too very long.

"So, what does it say?" I asked. "Can you explain its meaning?" I wanted to see if I could get her to verbalize it.

Her head dropped and she fell silent. She didn't want to offer any more. I tried another approach.

"Well, let's see," I began. "You use words like *hurt* and *painful*. I am guessing these refer to things that are too difficult for you to talk about, right?"

Her head nodded but she barely lifted her eyes to look at me.

"Even here? Remember, it's safe in here." My words were encouraging her to go on, but she either wouldn't or couldn't respond.

So, I continued. "The girls in the shadows, are they hiding? Their emotions or feelings?"

She nodded again. We were getting somewhere. "*Broken trust*," I ventured, "indicates someone in your past didn't treat you like they should have. Someone hurt you, right?"

The words produced an immediate reaction. She glanced at the door as if expecting something to happen, then looked at me and very slowly nodded. I had an impression that I had pressed her as much as I should so I handed the collage back to her.

"Thank you," I said. "If you would like to share another one next time I would be happy to see it." A small, almost imperceptible smile suggested that I would probably see another one before much more time passed.

The collage was the first tangible indication that Dani was dealing with some serious issues. There appeared to be an inner conflict regarding that which she could not talk about and those things she wished to share. It caused me to ponder about what could have happened to instill this emotional war within her. She was obviously afraid that someone might learn about our meetings and what was shared in them.

Over the next several weeks she brought several more collages. Each was totally unique and, yet, all had the same overall theme. Each portrayed pictures of men, women and children. Sometimes the women were in the shadows while others had little black rectangular pieces of paper carefully placed over their eyes and mouths as if preventing them from seeing things or even speaking about them. Each one was both interesting and dark. To me, the implied messages were both obvious and subtle.

Always on my mind was the realization that if Dani had been abused, I would need to report it to the proper authorities. As for reporting anything, I could only conclude that I did not know anything about anything. One thing I did know, she was a very complicated and troubled young lady.

As our interviews would draw to a close I would ask her to pray and she would always refuse. We talked about faith, prayer, and God and how God wanted each of his children to speak to Him in prayer. But each time she would refuse to even offer a simple prayer. It was difficult to gauge what she believed. Regardless of what she believed, we would end our sessions with me offering a prayer and a suggestion that she could also pray when she felt she needed strength and comfort.

After she left each session I was left wondering why she was still glancing at the door during our interviews.

CHAPTER 3

Finding Clarity Amid Chaos

When you come to the end of everything you know -
And the next step is into the darkness of the great unknown -
You must believe one of two things:
Either you will step out onto firm ground,
or that you will be taught to fly.
—Edward Teller
(Teller & Shoolery, 2002)

Why? Why was this happening? The question seemed to echo around the room unanswered. Everything was blurry. She couldn't make out faces or details. However, the pain was real. She lost count of the number of hits, then more pain! Why wouldn't it stop?

Then there was more pain, different pain. Only part of the blurriness cleared. It was much like looking too close through a magnifying glass. She could see a deep red liquid. Then it came to her, it was blood. Her blood! Fear and panic welled up inside of her. She tried to cry out for help but the words wouldn't come.

From some place came the voices; screaming at her, saying such horrible words. "You worthless piece of garbage!"

Then she felt a kick immediately followed by another.

"You worthless piece of garbage!" Again, there was a tremendous kick with a second right behind it.

"You are nothing, hear me? Nothing! You are less than garbage."

She did feel like garbage. Maybe the voice was right. Maybe I do deserve this. Then the screaming turned into a laugh. It sounded maniacal. It made her feel horrible and even more frightened. "You are so pitiful! Just look at you! Nobody will believe you. You are disgusting." The laughter faded slowly as darkness consumed her.

"You shouldn't have done that!" The voice was yelling again.

She couldn't remember what she had done.

"You broke the rules!" What rule did she break? She tried hard to remember.

Then without warning she received a punch in her stomach. She gasped for air but her lungs did nothing, seemingly paralyzed.

"I will teach you!"

Her mind was a blur now. She had no idea where she was yet the murky surroundings were somehow familiar.

Through the blurriness she saw the faintest flicker of light. She strained through the dark, billowing clouds storming through her head and through the almost unbearable pain to focus on that little light. Slowly the light began to grow. As the haze cleared she could see familiar surroundings. The bed stand, the lamp, the nightlight. She realized she was sitting on the floor in the closet looking out into her bedroom! As her heart rate slowed, she began to feel like herself once more, except for the ache in her stomach. She knew she would have that for the whole day.

Why was this happening to her? Why?

"Is it okay to not talk to someone on the phone when they call?" Dani asked this question and I almost didn't hear it. I refocused and took a moment to understand what she was really asking me. I caught myself from making a quick and witty retort. Certainly, this was so obvious it appeared to have a "No, duh..." kind of answer.

I was reflecting on our past several sessions. Dani demonstrated that she was comfortable during our meetings. She was talking more openly about her children: how they were doing at school, funny little pranks, frustrations, the games they played, etc. These were the normal things one would expect to hear about any family. On the outside, everything continued to appear normal. Seeing Dani at church or on the street, one would see a quiet young mom who doted over her children. The casual onlooker would never see that there was such an ocean of pain and emotion buried deep inside.

Slowly a visible transformation was taking place in Dani right before me. Her eyes radiated a light that had not been there before. Her hair was being washed frequently and she was conscientiously running a comb through it. Her deathly white complexion was replaced with a rosy color in her cheeks. Her speech carried a tone of confidence as she expressed herself. This was not the same young woman who had walked into my office on our first meeting.

Even with these dramatic and positive changes, the deep struggle within would make itself known in the matter of a moment during our interviews. Mood changes oscillated from confident and happy to withdrawn and fearful in just seconds. I still didn't know what caused these changes. Despite the fast-moving mood swings, she was spending more time exhibiting her newfound confidence.

"Excuse me?" I asked bringing my attention back to her question. "What did you say?"

"Is it okay not to talk to someone when they call on the phone? Is that being mean if I don't?" she asked again.

"Well, my dad always told me that you pay for the phone and if you don't want to talk to someone you don't have to." Her eyes let me know that I needed to explain more. "Dani, you are in charge in your home. You and Jeff pay the bills. If someone calls you on the phone, you can decide whether you want to talk to them or not. You decide. As to whether it is mean or not will depend on the perception of the person on the other end of the phone or the reason why you are doing it. You don't have to talk to anyone you don't wish to." This explanation seemed to satisfy her.

"Why, who is calling you that you don't want to talk to?" I asked.

"It's my mom and dad," she responded hesitantly. "They say such mean things to me. They yell at me and tell me everything I am doing wrong."

"It sounds like they might be a bit controlling. After couples are married, their parents are supposed to back away and let their children raise their own families. I think you can talk to whomever you like. Remember, Dani, you are in charge. Not your parents. You can decide what you want to do. Okay?"

"I can do that?" she asked innocently. "I can just not answer the phone?"

"Yes, you can," I replied. "But I have a better idea. Why don't you just have Jeff pick up an answering machine. Then, you can let the machine talk to them and you don't have to. If they leave a message you can listen to it if you want but you don't have to."

She smiled. "I like that. I will have Jeff pick one up."

Then she presented me another picture collage. This one seemed to be as dark and troubling as the others I had viewed. This one had images including a bedroom, garden, and trees. People, including young girls and babies, were placed throughout the scene. On each of them she had taken a black magic marker and drawn a line over their mouths and with some, also their eyes. There was a dad holding a little girl in his arms and the picture was torn so that the tear separated the two. A little girl with no eyes was holding her hand over her mouth as if keeping a secret. The most troubling of all was the picture of a large bloodshot eye with little words pasted over the pupil in bold letters: *HELP ME!*

As I handed back the collage, she asked what I thought. The reality of just how little I knew or understood about her situation bore into my heart.

"It looks like you spent a lot of time on this." I fumbled. She seemed pleased with my response.

"Do you want to see another?" she asked.

I really didn't. These works of art oozed messages of extreme hurt and pain. Setting personal feelings aside, I replied in the affirmative.

She carefully reached for her spiral book, flipped methodically to a specific page, folded the other pages under, and handed it over to me. She was being very careful so that I could not see any of the other pages in the book. There was a sense of 'mother bear' protection regarding those pages, as if they were of national security.

This picture was dark like the rest. The women all had a black line over their mouths. The man in the upper right corner appeared to be looking down at the women on the page. His eyes had been blacked out. Large words filled the middle of the page. *REMEMBER, HEALING THE CRUELEST WOUNDS* and *I CAN'T BELIEVE I LET SOMEONE DO THIS TO ME.* The giant words were begging to be heard.

"Do you want to talk about these?" I asked.

Her eyes flashed at the door and back to me again. Unmistakable fear was in her eyes and she instantly drew her legs up, locking her arms around them in an apparent attempt to provide herself with some protection. Without uttering a word, she shook her head.

Then, after a minute or so, she spoke. "I . . . I can't", she said. "This is why I create these." She held her spiral book close guarding it so no one might take it and learn its' cruel secrets. She moved towards the door as if to leave. I instantly knew the last question had been out of bounds.

"That's okay, you don't have to talk about them if you are not ready," I said reassuringly. "Maybe you can share another one with me next week. They really are quite remarkable," I added. Again, I winced at my struggle to find the right adjectives.

"I'd like that," she smiled. She quickly relaxed and her panicked breathing slowed. "Thank you for your time." She put her hand on the door knob to leave.

"Oh, Dani," I ventured, "I noticed you look at the door often. Are you expecting someone to be there?

"Yes," she responded; her head and eyes dropped.

"Who?"

She looked at me for nearly one entire minute, contemplating a response. Her eyes were wide with fear and her mouth opened as if she were going to respond, but without saying a word she turned and left my office.

It was almost dark when I left the building. As I locked the door behind me I had the distinct impression that I was being watched. I casually looked around the almost empty parking lot. The tall light poles illuminated puddles of light beneath each pole. I didn't see anyone lingering or waiting.

I did notice a car at the end of the parking lot that was backed in so as to have the front of the car facing the front door of the church. With a casual glance, I did not notice anyone sitting in the car. I chided myself for being paranoid. A neighbor must have parked the car there overnight or maybe they left church and walked home and forgot they had driven their car to the church. I shook my head at my foolishness and walked to my car, brushing aside any thought that I was the object of prying eyes or clandestine surveillance. Too many mystery novels, I thought. My growling stomach reminded me it was time to get home and eat some dinner. However, as hard as I fought against the idea, I still watched the rear-view mirror to make sure I wasn't being followed on the way home.

CHAPTER 4

Power and Control

Act in the face of fear
Get determination from failure
Be strong in hard moments
—From Dani's Diary

She couldn't breathe. "Why?" she asked herself. "What was wrong?" She gasped for air. Slowly it came and then it was gone again. Just as she was getting her breath she felt as though she got punched in the stomach. That was it, she was getting punched in the stomach over and over again. It was dark. So dark! She reached up to try to protect herself but it didn't seem to help. Then it stopped! She struggled desperately to stand.

Then came the yelling.

"You stupid idiot!"

"You worthless piece of garbage."

"Why do I have to put up with you?"

"You are ruining everything."

Those words were so harsh and painful. She kept racking her brain. "What did I do wrong? If I could just remember what I did wrong, maybe I could change and then I wouldn't get hurt anymore! Why can't I remember?"

Her frustration changed to terror as the voices stopped. She knew what was next.

"No," she tried to scream between gasping breaths. "Please no!" Then came the pain, excruciating pain. She fought back the screams. She knew if she screamed it would only get worse. Why didn't it stop? "Please God, please make it stop!" she prayed. "Or please just end it all and let me die. I can't take any more!" Then it welled up inside and was out of her control. She screamed!

As the scream left her lips she opened her eyes to find she was in the safety of her bedroom. Her house! As she fought to catch her breath she realized she was soaked in sweat. Her stomach hurt something fierce. But she was safe, in her room under her bed. The frightful images were just blurs. Why couldn't she see them clearly? Who were the people in them? Why do these dreams keep coming night after night?

The pictures that Dani showed me were disturbing; but not as troubling as the inference to the one that was her abuser. I saw and felt the fear. She was terrified. It wasn't evident at the time she came into my office or even when she left. It was usually at moments when she was either showing me something or thinking of telling me something which she could not talk about. Painfully I knew she was afraid to talk about whoever it was that frightened her.

During my teenager years I was smaller than most of the boys my own age, extremely skinny, and lacking in any self-confidence. In the junior high school I attended, there were two boys who seemed to have made it their life's work to terrorize me, perhaps because of my geekiness. I wore dark horned-rimmed glasses, and though the style has resurfaced to be popular and retro, it was the mark of death then. In my estimation, it was like putting a target on my back that said, "Nerd here, help yourself!"

These bullies would walk up behind me in the halls and trip me or maliciously knock my textbooks out of my hands. Every time it happened they were together. The two of them were a tiny gang and both were bigger and stronger than me. It was a case of being outsized and outnumbered. I wasn't big enough to fight one of them much less take the both of them on. During school hours, all I could think about was how painful it was going to be if they beat me up. So, each time I saw them coming down the halls of the school my knees went weak. Real fear came with the promise of real pain. I was sure from the outward signs during our visits that Dani must be experiencing the same type of fear that I had experienced. She was afraid of the consequence of telling. She was afraid of the pain.

I had guessed by now that Dani had been abused. Despite my suspicions, I didn't know for certain by whom, or what kind or why. Our most recent session shed some light on that. The images in the collages with the eyes and mouths blacked out were obvious representations that she was not able to speak about something in her past. Was it a family member such as her father that she was afraid of? Or someone else in her life? Since abuse appeared to be obvious from the collages, it was more than likely that her doctor had already filed a report.

I pondered what I should do. How should I proceed? I really didn't have any experience for this. I was not a trained psychologist, I had never been involved with abuse. Oh, my dad was kind of abusive when I was younger. He would yell and intimidate us. He even occasionally took a belt to us. But I really think that his real intentions were to help us learn right and wrong. I don't think he did it to gain some kind of sick pleasure from physically hurting us. His form of discipline was maybe excessive by today's standards, old school for sure. I remember being afraid of my dad until the day he died. Even then there were times I would feel the fear even after he had passed. He was a very confrontational and in-your-face kind of individual which may have been exaggerated by his military combat experience in World War II. Even today I remember some negative things my dad told me and the feelings I had when he said them. Maybe because of my age or that he was my father, they hurt and were burned into my soul. They became a part of me. If Dani had experienced this same kind of abuse or something much worse when she was a child, there existed the very real possibility that she was still suffering from the effects of that abuse now.

Remembering back, almost a year ago, I had attended a multi-denominational meeting on abuse in our community. I had received some materials about abuse, its effects on the victims, and how to recognize abuse in families. Now, I was struggling to find the handbook we had received. Feeling somewhat embarrassed, I remembered thinking I would never need those materials because this type of thing does not happen in our neighborhoods. Now I was faced with a reality that it did happen, and in my neighborhood.

Later that week, after rummaging through my filing system, I found the information given out at the conference. It was a formidable booklet of fifty or sixty pages stapled together, entitled *Working with Victims of Domestic Violence and Their Abusers* (2004). As I started reading through it, I found some appalling statistics. In 2003, in my state alone, there were over 10,929 child abuse or neglect victim cases reported. This number was staggering to me. I realized that these were only reported cases. How about people like Dani? How many go unreported? How many victims are there who are too frightened and terrified to come forward? Reported days of shelters used by victims of abuse indicated 53,023 per year. These were people who had experienced enough violence at the hands of someone else that they needed to get away from the abuse. Generally, they found refuge in a shelter because they had nowhere else to go. Again, the thought nagged at me: What about those that are too young or too scared to walk away? The staggering reality started to overwhelm me.

A heading entitled "Understanding what motivates an abuser – power and control" caught my eye. It listed a profile of an abuser. The notion of having power over others was very interesting to me because of the prominent religious communities within our state.

The booklet listed the following as parts of this profile:

- The abuser is typically a man and is most likely a father or husband although women can be abusers too.
- He thinks that he has the right and that violence is justified as part of his role.
- He feels entitled to use force.
- In some cases, he has learned this behavior in his past as an abused child or by witnessing parental abuses.
- This behavior works for him. Even if at some level he knows it is wrong, he justifies this behavior.

- His behavior is under his own control. He chooses when and where to abuse, and what parts of the victim's body he hits to hide the evidence from others.
- He chooses to direct his violence only towards the victim or those whom he perceives may be helping her.
- His need to control family members may increase with stress in his life. (p. 11).

The items in this list made sense. The abuser would feel justified due to his role as husband or father or parent. He would have to control his victim so that they would not report him or tell others of the abuse. He would have to protect his abusive behavior because at some level he (or she) would know the actions were wrong and could bring consequences of arrest or even jail. Yes, it would become all about power over his victim and control over his surroundings. Not only was there a victim, Dani, but there was an abusive person out there that needed to understand what he was doing was wrong and also that he needed God's help.

During our next meeting, Dani seemed troubled and looked as though she was afraid to ask something. I assured her again that she could tell me anything and that this was a safe place. About a half an hour went by when she finally began to open up.

"I need help" she said simply.

"In what way?" I asked. "How can I help?"

She was wearing a long sleeve shirt and her blonde hair had returned to looking untidy and appeared to have been brushed hastily. Her shirt was buttoned up to the neck and around each cuff. It hung somewhat tent-like on her. Slowly she unbuttoned her sleeve and carefully rolled it up a few inches to reveal a bandage on her arm. There was a spot where the blood had seeped through. The bandage was still bright red and it was obvious that this was a recent cut or injury.

"Are you okay?" I asked concerned. "What happened?"

"I cut myself," she said simply. She said it in a matter-of-fact way much like telling me what she had for breakfast.

"Did you have an accident?" I asked. Then I remembered she had mentioned that she needed help with cutting. That was months ago and I thought that had been resolved with her doctor.

"Hasn't your doctor helped you with that?" I asked.

"She doesn't understand." she replied tersely. "All she says is that I need more meds or stronger doses."

"She must be trained with this type of behavior," I replied, confident that her doctor was giving her the right type of help.

"I don't need more meds," she replied emphatically. "They make me groggy and my mind is fuzzy. I am just tired of being tired. My hair has been coming out in clumps and I am forgetting things. I just don't need any more meds, okay?" This sounded more like a strict command rather than a question needing an answer.

"But she must know what is best," I said firmly. "Maybe you should have somebody review your medications. Maybe there is a conflict with what you are taking. Just tell her that you don't want to take more medications." I paused and could tell she was processing my suggestion. "You could just tell her that you don't want to take them and see if she will help you without them."

After a moment, she replied in a sad and almost defeated tone, "I tried. But she said that all her patients must be on medications. She said that is how it helps them to deal with their trauma."

"She could be right. With her training, she has to know how to handle cutting and other problems." I was running out of things to suggest.

She started to break down. Tears were welling up in her eyes. She looked like someone sinking into quicksand in need of someone to throw a rope to her for help. "I am already taking plenty of medications. I don't need more. Don't you understand?"

"Okay."

This was the first time she expressed such strong emotion. She had been keeping her emotions so suppressed that I had thought she couldn't express them. Now she was crying out for help. I needed to throw her a rope of hope.

"I think I understand what you are trying to tell me. Let's go ahead and talk about it. First, tell me why you are cutting."

She wiped her tears and sat up. She looked at me with interest as if to say, "Now we are getting somewhere." We both looked at each other in silence for several minutes. She appeared to be gathering her thoughts.

"It helps me deal with the pain." she said simply.

That response didn't make sense. "Are you saying that you are cutting yourself to create pain to deal with other pain?"

She nodded and then dropped her eyes to the floor.

"So," I continued, trying to understand, "the other pain is covered up or disappears when you cut yourself?"

She nodded. "The pain from cutting allows me to not focus on the things in my head."

That made sense. We all do it. Some of us exercise to the point of exhaustion to allow us to forget something painful. Some people go shopping while others eat (or overeat). The act of cutting just seemed to be much more extreme as well as dangerous. Then, again, what she was probably dealing with was extreme.

"What kind of pain are you dealing with?" I asked.

She looked at me with sad eyes. "I don't know."

"Then how do you know they are painful?" I needed to understand how it worked.

"There are things in my mind. They are painful. They hurt. I can't deal with them. I can't make them stop. Please," she pleaded, "please make them stop! Please!" Her voice trailed off with this mournful request for help, tears again welling up in her eyes.

"Can you describe what kind of things," I asked.

"I don't know. They are clouded and blurry. They are like shadows moving, yelling. I hear horrible things. I can't make them out but I can feel the pain."

"You can feel the pain?" I asked. "From these, ah . . . thoughts in your mind?"

"Yes," she replied. She had her arms wrapped around legs which were drawn up to her chest. She was barely looking at me over her knees and her voice was so soft that I had to strain to hear her. "They come at night mostly. The shadows come . . . they yell at me . . . they hurt me . . ." Her voice trailed off and the room became silent.

She kept her gaze on me and I felt that my facial expression was being evaluated. There must have appeared some skepticism because she reached down and slowly pulled up her shirt revealing her stomach and ribs. Her stomach was slightly extended but her ribs were protruding through the skin revealing what I had already deduced . . . she was extremely underweight. But what really startled me was seeing black and blue skin discoloration all over her ribs.

"That looks painful," I exclaimed wincing. "How did that happen? Did someone do this to you?"

Lowering her shirt, she told me that the bruises came as a result of the images in her mind that came to her during the night.

"These images," I continued, "are they dreams? Or nightmares?"

Dani considered the question for a minute before responding. She replied, "Neither."

I was surprised and confused. I recalled hearing once of a person's memories being so real that they suffered injuries or exhaustion, but at the time I didn't know if it could really happen.

"What do you think they are?"

"I don't know." Dani's eyebrows were pinched together in thought as she tried to put whatever it was into words. "All I know is that when they come, I can't control them. There is something familiar about them. It's like I almost know where I am and what is happening, but things are clouded over or in shadows. I can't see details, only images. I hear voices but can't tell who is speaking."

She paused once more. Tears glistened in her eyes and I could tell she was battling within herself deciding whether she should share more with me or not. Reaching a decision, she continued. When she did her words were slow and paced as if the memory of them was painful. "When these happen they always hurt. Someone is hurting me. When I wake up I always have these." With that she pointed to her ribs where the bruising was evident.

I closed my eyes and offered a silent prayer. My mind raced to find answers that weren't there. I needed help. Help for Dani. The thought came to me that maybe these were memory fragments or traumatic memories. Just maybe her memories were so traumatic that she buried them so that she could not remember the details. Could it be that her mind was blocking these memories and now they were trying to get out so she could deal with them? Perhaps the doctors, in an attempt to help her, were prescribing too many medications, thus hindering her ability to deal with the pain and these memories.

"So, you are saying that these, let's call them 'bad memories', are causing bruising on your ribs?" I asked trying to keep any skepticism out of my tone. Her eyes indicated that she felt I might be understanding what was happening to her. "You go to bed at night with no bruising and wake up with the injury?"

Again, she nodded. She was looking intently into my eyes assessing my questions.

"Do you believe me?" she asked.

"Yes, I do." I responded reassuringly. The interesting thing was that I did believe her. In all the time I had worked with her, she had never been deceptive in any way. It was almost as though her emotional growth had stopped somewhere in her childhood. She was very believable.

The office was quiet for several minutes. The constant ticking of the wall clock was the only sound within the office. She was studying me, probably calculating whether she could trust me completely. Finally, her legs dropped to the floor, she squared her shoulders, and spoke with confidence.

"Can you help me? Can you help me to get them to stop?"

Now it was my turn to pause. I had to contemplate what I was doing. Dani was in pain and struggling with a problem that was bigger than she was. She believed in God but didn't know who He was. She needed help and I was confident that God had brought us together for a reason. I also knew that there was a medical backup team working with her as well. I knew that with God's help I would know how to help her.

"Dani, I am going to do my best to help you." Even as I said the words I felt a strength start to well up inside me. I knew that God had heard my prayer.

She nodded with a slight smile on her face. It was not a smile of triumph but a smile of relief and joy.

"I know that cutting is not the best way to deal with the pain. I am sure that is why the doctor prescribes medications." Her eyes narrowed when I spoke about any new medications. "However," I continued, "let's see if we can find another way for you to deal with the pain."

"There is one thing I do know," I continued, "that red stuff called blood, that comes out each time you cut, is vital to your body for health and even life itself. It keeps you alive to be with your children. I think they need a mom more than you need to cut, wouldn't you agree?"

She nodded and I could see she was thinking about it. I wanted to give her a strong motivation for not cutting and the love for her children seemed to be the best.

"Tell you what," I continued, "at out next meeting you bring me the razor blades and I will keep them here in my office. If you need them you can have them back. In the meantime, let's talk about the things that are causing pain and see if we can help you deal with that pain without the cutting. Deal?"

Considering the offer, she watched me for a few moments. Slowly there came a little smile. "Deal," she said.

On our next visit, she handed me several shiny new razor blades that were the kind that go in box cutters. They were wrapped in a tissue. She had been true to our deal. Now it was up to me to help provide a solution that would give her the ability to never need them back. I opened my desk drawer and put them in the back. As I closed the drawer I wondered what I had gotten myself into. I said another prayer asking God for help. I figured that if God's help was ever needed, now was the time. She really needed His help. I really needed His help. I knew God always helped His children when they asked Him for it.

For the next several weeks she would call me whenever she felt like cutting. As one of her hidden memories would come, forcing her to deal with the pain and anguish of reliving it, she would call me and let me know that she would like the blades back. We would talk about it and discuss alternative ways of dealing with the pain. Once we both agreed to a new way to deal with her current pain, her resolve was renewed. Each time she gained a little bit more strength until she finally didn't need cutting as a "drug" for her problems. God was showing us a new path for dealing with the pain.

I never did need to return those razor blades. As far as I know she never needed them again. They serve as a reminder that any one of us can have destructive behaviors in our lives and that we can make big changes with the right kind of help and support. Sometimes we need someone to show us a different way to solve our problems.

CHAPTER 5

A New Dani Begins to Emerge

(With His healing, a new Dani is born)

> *Tears are good.*
> *God can translate tears into words,*
> *desires and the intent of your heart.*
> –From Dani's Diary

By the time she heard the footsteps coming it was too late! She had purposely slept sitting up so she could be ready, but she had fallen asleep. She was so tired. So hungry! She couldn't remember when she had eaten last. She tried to wake up, to be ready. The door opened, strong hands grabbed her ankle before she could fight back. She was being dragged off her bed! As she was being dragged across the floor she looked down and saw that her nightgown was bunched up under her arms. The pain from the floor burns shot up her leg and back. She rolled, twisted and kicked but it had no effect. She almost relaxed then realized what was coming. The stairs! She tensed as her body, then her head pounded fiercely on each stair as she was dragged down them feet first. She saw stars through the tears and the pain in her head. Reaching the last step, the bumping stopped.

A New Dani Begins to Emerge

She was dragged into a closet in the basement! Why? What had she done?

She couldn't remember what she could have done to be put in the basement. She felt a sharp pain in her stomach. Another! She tried to deflect the kicks. They were painful and relentless.

"You worthless piece of garbage!"

"You are just a mistake! That is all you are. A mistake!" She didn't know if it was the volume of the yelling or the words that hurt the most.

"Why don't you just die!" One more kick to the stomach, then the door closed.

Her nightgown had been taken away. She felt cold in her underwear! The concrete was soaking up whatever warmth she had. There were no blankets, nothing to give warmth or comfort. Closing her eyes, she felt the ache in her midsection from the kicks.

When she opened her eyes again she was in her home, under her bed. She felt the warmth of her soft flannel pajamas and they were comforting. She was relieved that she was home, it was another dream. Why won't they stop! Was it real? The pain in her stomach seemed to confirm it was more than just a dream.

One of the things that I had begun to understand about Dani was that nobody believed her. Her husband seemed very apathetic. The doctors appeared to be more concerned about controlling her with drugs than finding the source of her troubles. On top of that she didn't trust very easily. Her weight loss and the cutting were evidence of cries for help that were going unanswered. I concluded that I must believe what Dani was telling me. She desperately needed someone to believe her but more importantly to believe in her.

Two events happened at about the same time that appeared to be defining moments in working with Dani. I didn't realize the connection at that time, but looking back they were like glaring road signs illuminating a highway at darkest night. They are essential to understanding Dani, her progress, and the changes in her frame of mind.

The first event was the most astonishing to me.

When Dani entered my office for a session I noticed something different about her. She looked to have more energy. Dani was directing her gaze into my eyes and she was smiling. Her posture was more confident and poised. Her blonde hair was neatly combed and hanging on her shoulders instead of being pulled back into a ponytail. I was looking at a new Dani and I marveled at the transformation.

"Guess what I did?" Dani asked the question with a hint of seeking my approval.

"I cannot begin to guess," I responded, "What did you do?"

"I fired my doctor," she replied.

Her comment took a minute to sink in fully.

"You did what?" I exclaimed. "You fired your psychiatrist? Why on earth did you do that?"

She explained what had transpired on her recent, regularly scheduled visit to see her psychiatrist. Dani expressed her desire to try living her life without taking any prescribed medications. The doctor had shut her down, insisting that she had to be on some medications in order to even meet with her. Dani had insisted that she wanted to try giving up ALL medications. The doctor refused. She repeated her protocol that all of her patients had to be on medications. She further explained that it was necessary for each patient to have these medications in order to get through the emotional stresses of what they were experiencing. The doctor concluded by insisting that there was no way she could do it on her own without the medications and she wouldn't be able to help her without them.

"So," she said, "I fired her."

I could not resist the inclination to smile as I imagined the sight of this petite little gal standing up to her medical Goliath and delivering to her one small stone from Dani's slingshot telling her she was fired. Before me Dani stood determined and confident that her decision made during the battle for self-control was right.

"Maybe they know something we don't. Maybe you need these medications to help you. As you know, I am not a doctor, nor do I pretend to be, and they know much more about this than I do." I commented.

A New Dani Begins to Emerge

"I have been on medications my whole life. I cannot remember a time that I was not on some type of medication. Either ones my parents were giving me or ones that the doctors were prescribing. I just want to know what it is like without drugs! Do you understand? I just don't want to take them anymore! I don't want to walk in a fog anymore!" The determination and strength in her voice was enough to let me know that I, too, would lose this battle if I attempted to fight it. Considering her renewed countenance, emotional strength, and confidence, this was a battle I was more than happy to concede.

"So, I fired my doctor and threw away all my meds," she concluded.

It occurred to me that if she had been on medications her whole life that she must have experienced some sort of detoxification and gone through this process since our last meeting.

"How have you been feeling since I saw you last?" I asked.

"It is interesting that you asked," she replied. "I have not been feeling very well at all!"

"Were you sick?"

"Yeah. I was really sick for several days. I think I had the flu."

"Did you have chills and shakes?" I questioned, feeling concerned.

She perked right up. "How did you know?"

"I would bet that you must have been going through withdrawals from all the drugs you were taking."

She thought for a minute and nodded. "Now, that makes sense." she said. "It didn't even occur to me. I just thought I had the flu or something."

The second event was rather disturbing.

At the end of each of our sessions I would ask her to pray. She would always refuse. I knew that the best way for her to start healing would be to pray and involve God by directing her faith toward Him. She always seemed to sense the moment approaching and would always be ready with her response of "I would appreciate it if you could do that," or she would tell me ahead of time "I don't feel like praying today." I was determined that somehow, I would get her to pray.

"Dani, I would like you to pray before you go. Can you do that please?" I surprised her by asking at the beginning of the session instead.

She looked at me thoughtfully for a few minutes. Visibly she was working through some thoughts and emotions. I decided to let her take as long as she needed. She looked at the door a couple of times. She looked down and then said, "I am afraid."

"Why are you afraid, Dani?" I asked.

She was afraid, I could see it in her eyes. She sat for several minutes, quiet, thinking. Then she said something that was somewhat of a breakthrough.

"Can I tell you why I am afraid? Is it safe?"

I spent the next few minutes reassuring her that it was indeed safe and that everything we talked about would be safe.

Again, she sat there, deciding if it was alright to share or not. Finally, the break-through moment arrived.

"I was not allowed to pray growing up." She said it quietly, her hesitation revealing her fear in telling me. "I remember kneeling down beside my bed to pray like I was taught in Primary." I could see tears welling up in her eyes as she was remembering not just the moment but also something painful. "I didn't hear him come up behind me, but I felt a sharp pain in my back." Her eyes were focused straight ahead as if she was looking right through me. "I looked up to find my dad holding a bat. He told me that praying was against the rules and if he ever caught me praying again he would hit me again only it would be much worse. He said girls like me weren't allowed to pray."

"Praying was against the rules?" I asked in astonishment.

"Oh, yes. It was against the rules. I have been afraid to pray ever since."

"Were there other rules?" I asked. Hopefully the shock I felt did not show on my face. I was trying to fully comprehend why her father denied her the right to pray.

She nodded. "I can repeat them from memory. He made sure I knew the rules and made me repeat them often."

This was the first confirmation that her father was most likely the one who had abused Dani. There was mental and emotional as well as spiritual abuse. To me, this act ranked right at the top of the cruelty list: to teach a child she couldn't pray.

A New Dani Begins to Emerge

I had expected her to display some great emotion in the telling of his rules, however, she repeated what she remembered with no outward emotion. Although nearly invisible, I could see the evidence of sadness and fear in her eyes.

"Dani, what were the other rules?" I asked again.

She looked at the door once more, looked down at her hands and didn't say any more.

After some patient encouragement Dani finally agreed to pray out loud. Her soft voice was almost inaudible, but her words clearly spoke the most humble prayer to a loving Father in Heaven I think I had ever heard. Her prayer, long overdue between a daughter and her Heavenly Father, brought tears to my eyes. I praised God silently in my heart for this significant breakthrough.

For weeks, I had been teaching Dani bit by bit about a God with everlasting love who loved each of His children. Dani, on the other hand, was teaching me about a whole new level of what abuse was. I was about to receive a complete paradigm change in my thinking. My world was about to change forever.

CHAPTER 6

Please Make Them Stop

"Look unto me, and endure to the end, and ye shall live; for unto him that endureth to the end will I give eternal life."
—Jesus Christ - 3 Nephi 15:9

A bump awoke her. How long had she been in there? She didn't know. All she knew was that it seemed forever. The rough occasional bumps and the closeness of the surroundings told her she was in the trunk of a car. The air was rank and smelled like exhaust. She couldn't tell whether it was day or night. It didn't make much difference to her. There was absolutely nothing she could do about it.

The car slowed. She tried to stretch and felt cramps in her legs and hips. She was wearing only a large t-shirt and the coldness brought giant goose bumps to her skin. The car came to a standstill. Next the engine stopped. She strained her ears to hear if any sound would betray anyone approaching the trunk. But all was quiet. Feeling sleepy she must have dozed off. Suddenly the trunk opened and a dark figure reached in and grabbed her hair and dragged her out of the car. She was only outside for a few seconds but it was enough to know that it was night.

She was pulled a few feet to a house and dragged inside.

"You are worthless," the gruff voice said. "You are a piece of garbage. You are a throwaway!" She felt a hit on the side of her head that sent her sprawling to the floor a few feet away. The hit was so sudden she didn't have time to react. Then she felt a kick. "If it was up to me I'd throw you in the dumpster. That's where you belong." Then she felt another kick, this time to her stomach forcing the breath out of her.

She started to cry, she couldn't help it. "Shut up!" the voice yelled. "If you cry I will make it worse for you!"

She stopped crying and clinched her teeth so that she wouldn't let out any sound. Then the kicks started again. She lost count of how many. She ached everywhere and wondered why it wouldn't stop. She tried to block her body from the blows with her arms and legs. It seemed to give her some protection but not enough to prevent the anger from manifesting itself in brutal and savage blows.

She opened her eyes just in time to see a foot coming straight at her head and then blackness.

Dani sat across from me. Once more she had drawn her legs up and encircled them in her arms. She must have had an extremely hard week. Her loose-fitting clothes could not hide how thin she was. Her arms had so little muscle. Even wearing tiny size jeans, her hips did not have enough muscle or fat to keep them in their proper place. Her face was a bit drawn, she looked quite pale and her hair was pulled back. Though the weather outside was warm she was wearing a long sleeve shirt. Again, it appeared that she was trying to hide how little weight her body carried. It was immediately apparent that whatever she was battling had set her back. I knew we had lost some ground.

"How have you been?" I asked trying to sound cheerful. She looked at me for a while and then answered softly that she was fine. There was sadness in her tired green eyes.

"I need your help" she whispered. "Can you please help me?"

"Of course," I said. "I am here to help you, Dani."

"I need to know it is safe. Is it safe?" again she looked at the door.

"Yes, Dani," I responded. "It is safe in here. You can say whatever you need to."

"And it won't go anywhere else?" she questioned. "You won't tell anyone? Promise?" She was pleading now.

"No, it won't go anywhere else," I said firmly.

"I . . . I . . . I have these dreams. They are like nightmares. They only seem to come in bits and pieces." She said it as though she was in real physical pain.

"They are never complete. It is almost like they are all jumbled up. I can't make any sense of it." She was almost panicked by it.

"What kind of dreams?" I asked.

"Bad ones," she said. "Real bad ones."

"When you say bad, does that mean bad things are happening to you?"

She nodded. She grabbed her legs even tighter.

"I wish they would stop. I can't sleep. They always seem to come when I am sleeping. They are horrible. I don't want to go to sleep anymore." She was really laboring with the thought of what she had been experiencing.

"I need to tell you something, but I am afraid you might laugh or think I am stupid."

"Dani, I would never think that. You can tell me anything."

She hesitated for a few seconds. "When I go to sleep at night . . ." She paused. She was having an inner struggle with some unseen force as if it wanted to prevent her from speaking.

"I always wake up in a cold sweat. Jeff has stopped sleeping in the bedroom because he says that before I wake up I am screaming. He sometimes wakes me up and tries to help me. I just don't know what to do." I could tell she wanted to cry but she fought back the tears. "And there is something else . . ." she hesitated again, fearful to continue.

"Sometimes when I wake up" she ventured sheepishly, "I find myself under the bed. Other times I end up in the closet." This wasn't even close to the answer that I had anticipated.

"Why under the bed?" I asked.

"Because it is a safe place." She responded so matter-of-factly that it sounded as if it was the most logical response possible.

Then it dawned on me. "Did you use to hide under the bed when you were younger so you wouldn't be hurt?" I asked.

She nodded a 'yes'.

I could only imagine her, frightened, hiding from someone under her bed. What a life for a child.

I sat and thought about what she had told me. What could I do? This was definitely beyond my abilities.

"Maybe now is a good time to go see a psychiatrist." I ventured.

"NO!" She suddenly came alive. "I won't go back to her!"

"Well, if not her, there are other . . .". She didn't even let me finish the sentence.

"I don't want to see any doctors. They all want me to take medications. I won't go back to taking the meds."

"But these doctors are trained to help with these types of things. They can help you."

"I won't go," she said defiantly.

"But Dani," I protested, "I don't have the training for this. I am not a doctor or psychiatrist."

"You work for God, don't you?" she asked.

"Well, yes, I do." I replied.

"You told me that God had great power to work miracles, didn't you?"

I felt convicted by my own words. "Yes, Dani, I did say that," I agreed.

"Then God will tell you how to help me. I know He will help you. God will tell you what to do."

As I looked at her across the desk, I recalled a Scripture from Matthew in the New Testament:

> *When Jesus heard it, he marvelled,*
> *and said to them that followed, Verily I say unto you,*
> *I have not found so great faith, no, not in Israel.*
> –Matthew 8:10 KJV

Dani had this kind of faith. I marveled at her great faith and trust in me. I reached out to God at that moment and sought His help in her behalf.

"Okay, Dani. I will try. If you have this much faith in God, I know He will help us."

She smiled. It was a pretty smile as well as a rarity. Her eyes brightened and some of the tiredness left her eyes and was replaced with tears. This time they were tears of joy.

"Alright, tell me about these dreams."

Dani described her dreams. As she did so, they seemed to be more like memories but she couldn't be sure. She thought they might be memories from her past. She described them in fragments: yelling, screaming, shouting, and hitting. The only conclusion she could draw was that it was her father and mother and maybe someone else, it just wasn't clear. She was frustrated because as hard as she tried she couldn't remember the details. In each memory, she was a child or in her youth. One thing that each memory fragment had in common was that for Dani, they were very real.

"When they come," she continued, "I can remember some things very clearly: smells, touch, sounds. I know it sounds crazy, but I cannot remember where I was or who was doing it. And when I get kicked or beat, it is just like it is happening to me all over again. I have even woken up with bruises in places where I was hit or kicked during the dream the night before."

I remembered hearing about those type of dreams. But from where? I had to think for a few minutes and then it came to me. My uncle! He had served in World War II in Iwo Jima. I remembered him describing some of his experiences. He had told me how horrific some of the battles had been. He remembered seeing most of his buddies being blown apart or maimed. He said that in some of these memories he could remember the fear, the smell of the sulfur, the screams of the men, the sounds of incoming artillery shells, and the smell of burning flesh. He remembered them just as though he were there. I remembered that they called it PTSD or Post Traumatic Stress Disorder (during World War I and II, it was called shell shock).

If my uncle had such exact recall, then her description of the dreams made sense. I had only heard about these types of experiences in relation to men in wartime situations and never with non-wartime experiences. However, it made logical sense that if someone like Dani had experienced traumatic events they should affect the body and mind in the same way.

"Do you think I am crazy?" she asked.

I thought for a moment and then responded, "No, I don't think you are crazy." I said the words clear and distinct with conviction. I really didn't think she was crazy at all. "Thank you for sharing this with me. I know it must have been difficult and I think this will help us to figure out what happened in your past so we can help you."

What I had just said seemed rational to me, but I found myself feeling at a total loss regarding how I was going to help her. I felt some comfort in the fact that she had so much faith that God would help me to help her. With faith like that I had greater confidence.

Then I remembered something. "Before you leave I have a suggestion for you. I would like you to try what I call the Bubble Effect."

Dani looked at me quizzically. "What is the Bubble Effect?"

This must have been heaven-sent inspiration since I did not come prepared to share this idea. It simply popped into my mind just at that precise moment. The Bubble Effect was a technique someone had taught me years ago when I was battling outside influences such as annoying people or difficult circumstances or when I was losing focus and being sidetracked. The technique was simple and required that you imagine a bubble surrounding you, and then, as something happened, like some annoying person was draining your energy, you imagined that their words bounced off the bubble before they (the words) reached you. This way not only the words but the emotion with the words would be deflected and would leave you without the emotional impact. Odd as it may sound, it had really worked for me.

Dani smiled while thinking about it for a minute. Making sure she understood the technique she then agreed to give it a try. I had seen her smile twice in one day, it was a blessing to see. We agreed to meet in another week and she quietly slipped out the door.

After Dani left that evening I cleared my desk and got ready to go home. I was mentally and emotionally exhausted. I was also somewhat lost about how to proceed as well. As I started to leave I had a feeling that I had something left undone. Turning back to my desk I knelt down and poured my heart out to God for help and for Dani.

CHAPTER 7

The Flood Gates Open

The right kind of change doesn't take you away from yourself; It awakes you up to yourself.
—From Dani's Diary

The air was thick and musty. Small pinpricks of light came in through the metal wall of the shed. She could tell by their intensity that they were from the full moon that hung in the night sky. Aside from what little moonlight managed to illuminate the interior of the shed, she was alone.

How long had she been there? It could have been minutes or hours. Her arm ached and was cramping near her shoulder. She pulled on her arm again trying to free it, but the restraint around the wrist held tight. Her hand was tied to something above her head which kept her arm raised at an uncomfortable upward angle. Her legs were tired from standing so long. The height of her tethered wrist allowed her to slightly bend her knees but did not allow her to sit down. At one point, she had started to fall asleep only to be awakened by a wrenching pain in her shoulder. She wanted to cry out in pain but something inside her told her that was a mistake, a painful mistake, so she consciously chose to just whimper quietly.

She remembered it was summertime. However, the night was cold. She felt it so much more standing there in only her underwear. Her bony body shivered from the chill. She wished she were in her bed under the warm covers sleeping. Why was this happening?

She heard a door open and close in the distance. Her heart leaped with hope. Someone was coming to help her, to free her, and take her to her bed. She heard someone fumble with the chain and lock on the shed door. The doors opened wide and the moonlight silhouetted the frame of a person who took up most of the door. Her heart sunk as realization set in that this was not a rescue.

"So, you thought you could get away with it, did you?"

She tried to think about what he was talking about but couldn't recall what she could have done.

"I told you that you were to keep the secret. But I found out that you tried to tell someone. You ARE a worthless piece of garbage."

In the dark she had no warning as she felt a punch in her stomach. Her air was expelled and she desperately struggled to breathe. Then she heard a tool scrape from nearby. The she knew what was happening. She struggled to get her arm free as she felt the first blow from a metal object, some sort of tool she couldn't identify. Then she felt another and another. The pain was unbearable - so much so that she cried out.

She heard a low growl from the figure. He fumbled about on the shelf then she heard a tearing sound and a wide piece of tape was put over her mouth. She tried to scream but the sound was muffled as blow after blow connected with her bare exposed body. She prayed it would stop. She tried to be brave. She used all her strength to remain standing and then everything went black.

When she awoke she lay sweating in a corner wedged up under her bed. How did she get there? She looked down to find herself dressed in her flannel nightgown. She was relieved. It was only another nightmare. Oh, how she ached! Her stomach, her arms, and legs throbbed where she had been hit. Or had she? She wished these nightmares would stop. She laid down where she was and sobbed.

The chapel was relatively quiet except for the occasional cry of a restless young baby or the impatient protests of a bored child. To help maintain the expected reverence, conscientious parents cradled their antsy little ones, squeezing past other worshipers to slip out of the meeting as unnoticed as possible through the double doors into the hallway.

The speaker was a bit monotone. A few worshipers dozed off. Sitting on the stand with the podium obstructing part of the congregation, I couldn't positively conclude if it was the speaker making them drop off or whether the air conditioning just couldn't keep them cool enough because of the heat of the summer day.

The talk being orated over the pulpit was really quite good. The speaker, an older balding man, had a pleasant grandfatherly look as he told a story, a miracle really, about his father. He exercised great faith in overcoming a life-threatening situation which resulted in his father saving the life of his son, the speaker. A miracle was just what I needed right now.

As I observed the congregation from my assigned place before them, I could see the families I had come to know and love. Each one had a story and none were without some challenge or difficulty in their lives. However, just by looking at them, their appearances would not give any indication of their own personal struggles. Their countenances appeared worshipful and intent on listening to the message being given. The same was true about the young lady who became the focus of my attention at that moment.

Sitting in the middle of a pew about halfway back in the chapel was Dani and her family. She was flanked on each side by her children while Jeff was sitting a foot or so away from them quite oblivious to his family. He was focusing his attention on the speaker. Dani was being a typical mother, seeing to the needs of her children and imploring them to be reverent. I was impressed to see how much she lovingly responded to their fidgeting and irritation with each other. Her ministrations were not forced or mechanical. She really loved her children.

The casual observer would be completely unaware of the hurricane-force turmoil that she had going on inside. To me she appeared even thinner. There was no doubt within me that it was a result of her internal struggle combined with her eating disorder. There were dark half-moon shapes under her eyes; the result of lack of sleep.

I found myself thinking back over our interviews. Everything I had tried so far had only given her short-term relief from her nightmare chaos. She had told me at our last interview that the nightmares were getting stronger and building up in her mind like a dam ready to burst. The Bubble Effect worked for a while until these memory fragments came crashing through with more power than she could resist. They were still indiscernible and without any true clarity to her. The physical toll on her was obvious and I knew something life changing needed to happen soon. I closed my eyes and silently offered a prayer. I pleaded with God for an answer to find some way in which I could help Dani.

As I heard the speaker conclude his talk I saw in my mind a scene from an old television newscast of the Teton Dam in Idaho in June 1976. The dam had given way and in my mind's eye I could see the water flow. Although the initial force of the water was highly destructive as it broke through the compromised dam, the image of the water spreading out over the farmland appeared to be somehow peaceful.

After the closing hymn was sung and a prayer was offered, I wondered why the thought of the bursting Teton Dam came at that moment. Trying to determine its significance was put aside as I became busy with the usual duties that needed to be performed on a typical Sunday.

"I don't think I can take much more of this," Dani said with resignation as well as emotional and physical exhaustion. She was really trying hard to put on a good front but she looked gaunt as if she probably wasn't eating well. Her eyes seemed to have a hollow look. Sitting there her posture indicated surrender. She had all the indications of someone who was about to give up.

"Tell me what has been going on," I ventured, knowing that we were at a crossroads. I knew if something didn't change I would be forced to call in medical experts or the authorities.

"I can't shake these nightmares. They just keep coming no matter what I do. I can't sleep. I can't eat." She spoke in short staccato-style sentences almost like she were running out of energy.

I wanted to go around the desk, put my arm around her and comfort her but I had known from the beginning of our meetings that I needed to keep a distance in place so she could never ever question my motives or my intentions. Suppressing the charitable inclination, I remained where I was in my chair.

"Can you describe them to me?" I asked.

She looked at the door again. I had gotten used to this but this time there was real fear in her eyes.

"I can't tell," she said emphatically. "I am not supposed to tell."

"What do you mean you aren't supposed to tell?" I countered.

"I was told not to tell. If I did, bad things would happen."

"Who told you Dani? When were you told not to tell?" I asked, so anxious to finally get some much-needed answers. An honest answer might just be the key to help her at last.

As she looked at me tears welled up in her eyes. This was another rare emotion expressed by Dani. Her emotions were always so carefully guarded. To see her this way almost broke my heart. She was struggling and reaching out for help and I felt like I was letting her down.

In answer to my question she said simply, "I don't know."

"You don't know?" I asked.

"They are just voices yelling at me. Saying such harsh and mean things. They said I am disgusting and worthless. They said if I tell, terrible things will happen."

"What kind of terrible things?" I asked.

"I don't know. It is blurry and jumbled. I can't make it out. I have been trying to push them away but they are too strong."

She hung her head. The silence stretched out the time making it seem like hours instead of minutes. The tick-tock of the battery-powered clock on the wall magnified the silence. A motorcycle passed by the building sounding like a large bumble bee. Without knowing why, I deliberately allowed the silence to fill the room. My silent prayers were heard and a peaceful calm feeling filled the room. I could tell that Dani could feel this as well because she raised her head, squared her shoulders, and looked me in the eye.

"I am sorry for complaining," she said as she showed she was back in control again.

"Don't be sorry," I said. "I get the impression that you've never been able to share your feelings freely and openly."

She nodded in agreement.

"While you are in this room Dani, you can feel free to share your thoughts and feelings without criticism or reprisal."

She looked at me quizzically as if not believing what I was saying.

"I mean it, Dani." I tried to say it with empathy and kindness.

She smiled. Once again, her green eyes sparkled with hope and faith. She seemed to have more energy.

"Do you mind if I tell you more?" she asked.

"I don't mind at all."

"When they come, I hear voices yelling mean and horrible things." Her voice faltered. She hesitated. "It feels like it is really happening. The words are telling me not to say anything. I can't! Don't you see? If I say anything there are consequences."

"Who is telling you these things?" I asked.

"I don't know."

"When did this happen?" I continued to ask.

"I don't know." she said emphatically. "I just don't know!"

She was obviously not saying anything out of fear of what could happen to her. Maybe the nightmares or memories were being blocked. If they were being blocked out, it could be like they were dammed up inside. The longer she seemed to keep them bottled up inside the worse it was getting. Efforts to cause them to be destroyed or obliterated just weren't working. I felt again the sense of being at a loss of how to help her.

Dani was really struggling and was at her limits both physically and emotionally. Her refusal to take medications seemed to cripple my ability to offer any obvious viable solutions. She needed help and she needed it now.

As I sat there struggling in my mind what I should do, the images of the Teton Dam came back to me. Maybe holding back the memories or trying to suppress them was not the answer. Maybe allowing them to come, much like the flood waters flowing over the farmlands, was the answer. At least we would know what we would be dealing with.

"Dani," I ventured, "maybe we have been going about this the wrong way."

"What do you mean?" she asked.

"What we have been trying to do is suppress the memories or even destroy them. Right?"

"That's right," she responded. "I have tried to do everything you have asked." Her eyes had a trace of pleading. "Haven't I been doing good enough?" Dani didn't accuse me of being shortsighted or lacking inspiration, instead she was blaming herself for something that neither of us fully understood.

"Yes, Dani, you have been doing very well. It is just that I think I am letting you down. I am sorry."

She looked at me with wonder and surprise. Noticing her expression, I tried to think back over what I had said. Had I offended her? Was she shocked at something I said?

"Dani, why are you looking at me that way?" I asked.

"It's just . . . just that . . . no one has ever said that to me before," she responded.

I let that soak in for a minute. I had said 'I am sorry'. I wondered how many times I had said those words in my life and how diluted it may have become to me in my everyday speech. For her it was truly the first time it had been said to her. That realization tore at my heart.

"Dani, what I was trying to say is that maybe instead of holding the memories back, we need to let them come. Whatever comes, I promise you, I will be right here to help you with them. Okay?"

She thought for a minute as if testing the idea. Obviously, the other way wasn't working. She needed hope and relief.

"What if it is too hard? What if I don't want to know?" She seemed to be backpedaling now.

"Well, what we have been doing hasn't been working. We have no idea what we are dealing with. As it stands you are losing weight and it probably won't be long and you'll be in the hospital or something and most likely back on medications."

Her face indicated a real internal struggle while she was weighing the options.

"On the other hand, Dani, if they come, we will at least know what is causing all these nightmares. We can deal with the truth. And I will be right here to help you. This way we may be done with all of this in a week or so and then your life can get back to normal."

She looked up at me with her vibrant green eyes, suddenly full of hope.

"Okay," she said. "I will do it."

As Dani left my office I felt sure we had found an answer to a prayer. A subtle realization came to me at that moment. God had provided a way for Dani to bury these horrible experiences so that she didn't have to deal with them while she was a child. Now that she was an adult she would be more equipped to deal with them. I was recognizing another miracle from God.

Several days passed without word from Dani. There hadn't been many calls from her between our appointments, but considering the circumstances I anticipated receiving an emergency call, but none came. I started to feel somewhat unsettled and decided to call her.

I made the call but there was no answer. Knowing she was a busy mom with kids in school and running a household, it didn't cause me any worry. I would try again another time.

Later that night my family had just finished dinner and I was just settling down to relax with them and play a board game. My cell phone vibrated indicating there was a new text message. The two words on the screen sent my heart racing.

"HELP. PLEASE."

CHAPTER 8

A Normal Beginning

". . . there are many angels standing behind you all the time." They are guiding you through this time in your life. *"They are here to help you."*
—From Dani's Diary

Shortly after receiving her text I made my way to my home office. After closing the door, I called her. There was instant regret and self-reprimanding for suggesting to her that she should allow the memories to flow freely. It had felt like a prompting and the right thing for her to do. Now, hearing her frightened voice, I theorized that I had done the wrong thing.

"This is too hard. Too difficult. I can't do it alone!" Dani was stressed and sounding quite panicked.

"Slow down, please. What is too hard and too difficult?" I asked.

"I received a memory last night. I did like you suggested and I let it come. It is horrible. I can't understand it."

"Remember, Dani, I told you I would help you with them. Can you tell me about it? We can go over it right now."

"No. I can't," she said emphatically.

"Why?" I asked.

"Because I am afraid I will get in trouble," she replied.

"You aren't going to get in trouble," I shot back.

"Not with you," she retorted. "I can't do it over the phone."

"How about at my office? Will that work?"

"No!" was her simple and emphatic reply.

I guessed that she might feel uncomfortable in telling me in person or on the phone because the memories were graphic in nature.

"Will you agree to meet with me tomorrow night?" I asked.

The line was silent. I listened intently then heard a deep breath on the other end of the phone. It had an element of panic in it if that was possible.

"Okay," she answered. "I will be there."

"Can you wait that long?" I asked with concern in my voice.

"I think so," she replied and the line went dead.

When we met the next day, she brought me several items that she found in a box that had been packed and given to her when she got married and moved out of her parent's home.

The first was a journal written by her mother during her 'new mom' years. When I asked her how she got the journal she indicated that she had just found it in the box. Her mom had helped her move and she thinks it got put into the box by mistake. The journal was during a brief period of time when Dani was about five years old. Her mom had just had a new baby brother and she was writing about the family. Her comments were all accolades and wonderful experiences about Dani.

September 2

Dani was such a doll today. She helped out around the house and did everything I told her to do. I was afraid that she would have a difficult adjustment to her younger brother Eric. But she treats him with such love and concern. She wants to hold him almost too much. She coos and talks to him all the time. I am so blessed to have my little Dani.

October 19

Today I got overwhelmed in a big way. My husband has been going to school and working so hard and is gone most of the time. Last night I was up with Eric, he must have had a sick stomach. So this afternoon I sat down and started crying. Sweet little Dani came up and patted me on the shoulder and told me everything will be alright and that Heavenly Father loves me. She is such a joy to our family.

December 2

Today we had our first snow. Dani was so excited. I bundled up little Eric and we all went outside and made a snowman in the front yard. I took pictures of Dani putting the nose on the snowman. She was so cute. She gave the snowman a hug.

There were other entries in the journal. All were similar in nature and describing a wonderful, yet struggling family. When I asked Dani about some of the events, she said she did not remember most of them which to me was not too unusual. I didn't remember much of my younger growing up years either.

The second item that she brought me was a little red spiral notebook with *Dani 1st Grade, Age 5-6* written on the front. The book was filled with pages of block letters that appeared to be assignments given to her by the teacher at school.

August 30

It is the first day of school.

(Then there was a picture of a girl smiling and her name at the bottom of the page.)

August 31

I am Dani.
I am a girl.

Written at an angle before the word 'girl' was the word 'bad'. It seemed to have been added some time later. It was written using the same block letters. Below the writing was a picture of a girl holding a flower but her face was blacked out.

There were several more pages with writing, butterflies, pictures of flowers and shapes. I almost missed the significance of this page.

October 20

Dani wrote:
It is harvest time.
We made chains with patterns.
We had a super assembly.
(Below was a picture of a man with a mustache and it looked as though he had tears on his face.)

The journal contained many more similar pages telling of fall and Thanksgiving. Then I read the following:

December 10th

We made snowflakes.
We have Christmas games.
We made calendars for presents. Jimmy D. has been sick and we are making him a card.

(Below it she had drawn a picture of a girl lying on a bed with her face blacked out.)

There were pages with dates from January to June with activities in school from butterfly watching, to a cat having babies, flowers in the spring. All pages had drawings below the activities. As the entries continued, the pictures detailed more revealing images. The boys or men had mean expressions while the girls or women had Xs over their eyes and their crotches. I couldn't tell when the Xs had been added. The last page was the most disturbing. In a child's hand were printed the words:

June 2

We are reading in the Scriptures.
We are learning about Jesus.
We are learning.
We are saying a prayer.
We are talking to Jesus.

And then appeared two additional lines that were added in the same print style only slightly smaller in size.

Jesus doesn't like bad girls.
Jesus hates Dani.

This last sentence literally broke my heart. Seeing that this child believed that Jesus hated her was gut wrenching. How did she come to that conclusion? Was she taught that by someone?

I had occasion to read through the spiral book later. In fact, I did so several times, each time trying to find an answer. Was it really written by Dani when she was six years old? Or was it written by someone else. Or was it written by Dani later in her life because she was emotionally trying to explain what happened as a child. As I read more, I came to the realization that she had written it when she was in school during the first grade. I also concluded that the alterations must have been made after the teacher reviewed her work, reasoning that surely a teacher or school administrator would have seen the Xs over the eyes and genital areas in the drawings and the glaring declaration about Jesus at the end of the book. A responsible teacher would conscientiously have reported something to the authorities out of concern for the child.

I contemplated about who would have altered the book. It seemed most likely that Dani had put the Xs over the images and colored over the faces of the girls. My conclusion for the added marks must have been a subconscious attempt to cover the eyes and faces to prevent them (or herself) from seeing something terrible. It was her way of expressing that which she was unable to deal with or discuss with anyone else.

If her mother's journal was correct and the spiral book was also accurate, then obviously something must have happened during this period in Dani's life that caused so much pain to her then and now.

The third item she let me see was her personal and confidential diary. Within its pages were comments and quotes she had received from church members, clergy, and friends to give her encouragement and hope; people that knew something was wrong but not the details, who desired to help but did not know how. She shared with me some of her favorite ones that had given her strength.

When Dani had come into my office, she sat down and hugged her legs with her arms. After a few minutes of silence, she looked at me and spoke.

"I had a memory or a nightmare come last night. I want to share it with you. Please?" she asked hesitantly as though she expected me to say no.

"I would be glad if you would, if you feel comfortable enough to share it with me." I responded.

"But I can't. I can't do it here."

I was suddenly confused. "You want to share it but you cannot do it here?" I asked.

She hesitated, looked at the door, then around the room and then looked at her hands folded in her lap.

"Dani, what is wrong?"

Slowly she looked up and said, "I am afraid."

"Afraid of what?"

"That I will get in trouble." The response sounded a lot like what one of my kids would say when they thought I would get upset with them for something they did wrong.

"You won't get in trouble." I responded. "It will be just between you and me. How could you get in trouble?"

"Really?" she asked.

"Really."

"Okay, but I can't do it here."

"You mean you want to tell me but don't think you can tell me about it face to face?"

She nodded. "It is too embarrassing. Too difficult."

"I can understand that." I said with empathy.

"You do?" she asked.

"Yes, I do. But how can you tell me about it if you cannot speak it to me?" Hopefully this was not going to be a barrier to more progress.

"Can I ask you a question?" Dani looked sheepishly at me.

"Of course." I said.

"Can I email them to you? Would that be okay?"

Obviously, she had given this some thought. For her this was NOT to be face-to-face discussion. So, she had found a medium that would lessen the fear and anxiety, yet still allow her to communicate.

"That would be fine. I think that is a splendid idea." I reached for a piece of paper and wrote down my private email address and handed it back to her.

She smiled and told me she would send it right away.

"Can I ask you another question?"

I nodded.

"When I send it, can you help me understand it? Help me to handle it?"

"Yes, I will. I will do my best to help you."

We said a prayer before she left my office. I felt like I had made a major step in helping Dani. I said a prayer asking for God's help. He had given me so much inspiration up to this point and I was certain He would be essential in dealing with the things she was about to reveal to me.

It was the first day of kindergarten. Dani was so excited. She couldn't' believe she was actually there. She stood next to her dad as he was talking to the teacher. Then the teacher looked down at her. "Oh, what a beautiful child!" Dani couldn't believe she was talking to her. "I am glad you are here. I can see you and I will get along just fine! We will be great friends." Dani was overwhelmed. This teacher actually thought she was beautiful.

She had just gotten seated and looked around. She noticed her father had left. She started to relax. It was short lived, however, when a very serious looking man came to the door and called out her name. Her heart sunk. She stood up and followed the man out into the hall. Looking up she was terrified to see her father! The man told her that her father had requested she go to another class. She followed the man down the hall where she entered another door. Her new teacher looked overwhelmed getting one more student to an already full class. She took a seat. The rest of the day was a blur.

When she got home her father grabbed her arm and pulled her into his bedroom. After closing the door, he hit her on the side of the head. The blow caused her to stumble. He grabbed her arm and then punched her in the stomach. She panicked because she couldn't breathe. While fighting for breath he hit her again.

"You are not beautiful, say it!"

She tried to get the words out but she was hit again.

"You are not beautiful, say it!"

She struggled to say it.

"Nobody loves you or cares about you! Your teacher doesn't care about you. She doesn't have time for you! Understand?"

Another hit. And another. She started to cry.

"Stop crying! Don't be a baby!"

Another hit! Why didn't he stop? She hurt so badly!

"You are not beautiful. You are ugly and a worthless piece of trash. Say it!"

She said it.

"You are ugly and a worthless piece of trash."

It went on and on. She could feel the tears run down her cheeks. "Please, God! Make him stop! Please?"

The beating continued. She was thinking her father was right. God didn't come. He didn't rescue her. God must not love her after all. She was worthless! She felt like a piece of trash.

Dani started sending her memories. The first memory was of an experience she had on the first day of Kindergarten. I was appalled at the brutality of what she had described. I tried to perceive whether or not she had made the whole story up, but it was too exact to be anything but the truth. She described this memory in such detail and even included specific memories like smells and textures and emotions. She also indicated she even felt the beating just like she was living it all over again.

I tried to reassure her in my return email that this was not her fault. I felt it was important for her to know that. Surely when things like this happen, children blame themselves. Her over-controlling father meant to diminish her self-image and confidence thus preventing any attempt by her to speak with anyone about the things that happened to her at home. Also, it was obvious that her father had managed to move her to a more crowded classroom, to be left with an overwhelmed teacher. Such a situation would guarantee that a little troubled girl could easily be overlooked. Was this how people calculated to hide their abusive behavior?

Secondly, I let her know that this event had already happened. She had a hard time grasping this concept because to her if felt as if she were in Kindergarten all over again and it was happening now instead of in the past. Since she was experiencing it now she also felt that it was actually happening now. I had to continually remind her that this was something that happened many years ago. Once she caught the concept that this event had happened a long time in the past, she seemed relieved. I could tell she felt better by the end of the text messaging. I was grateful to have maneuvered through this crisis and help Dani recognize where the memory was in real time.

Even though she was now emailing me about the memories she was receiving, I still felt it was necessary to continue our regular weekly appointments.

As Dani sat before me during another visit, I could tell she was struggling with something.

"I just don't understand," she said in an absent-minded way, half to herself and half to the room around her.

"Understand what?" I asked, bringing her fully back to our current meeting.

"These memories are starting to flood into my mind." I wasn't lost to the flood reference and my Teton Dam revelation. "I just don't think I can keep up with them."

"I want you to know that I really appreciate the emails you have sent. I know how hard this must be for you."

She nodded in agreement.

"Have you been able to email me about each of the memories you are receiving?" I asked.

She shook her head with a negative response. I could tell she was getting overwhelmed. "By the time I can write all the details down and send it to you I may have received two more. They are not waiting to come at night anymore. I can be doing dishes or changing a diaper and I can receive another one."

"So, let me ask you a question. With the memories you have sent and my responses to try and discuss them with you, have they continued to bother you?"

She paused to consider the question.

"Come to think of it, no," she said, the realization of it surprising her. "No, they are not bothering me at all."

She gave me a weak smile. This was encouraging. I felt a touch of *joy*. The Lord was directing us with our new approach to the nightmares and the results were positive!

"But what I can't understand is . . ." Her voice trailed off suggesting that she was afraid to ask her troubling question.

I just let silence fill the room while she struggled with her thoughts.

"Why are they so painful?" she finally said, finishing her question.

Now it was my time to pause as I thought for a minute before responding.

"Dani, you know I am not an expert in this at all, but here is what I think. All these memories were of experiences from a long time ago. These were awful memories and I am sure that your young mind couldn't cope with them, so to protect you, your mind must have buried the whole memory with all the smells, pain, emotions, sounds, and everything. Kind of like a horrible home movie but with all the bells and whistles. These were stored because you could not handle them then."

"But why now?!" Desperation clung to her voice.

"Maybe God feels that after waiting all these years that now is the time for you to be healed. You may not have been in the right circumstances or environment for that to happen until now. You have to admit that you have been pretty darn miserable and it was getting worse. It was even affecting your health. At least now you have some details about what happened and together we can deal with what we know." It made perfect sense to me. She had been seeing images and hearing nameless voices and they were struggling to come out. Why now? Maybe God had prepared me to help her through this as well.

"But it is so hard!"

My heart went out to her. She didn't ask for this. She didn't choose to be abused. Unfortunately, she was suffering because of it. I could clearly see why she didn't understand. Why her? For that I didn't have an answer, at least not right now. Why do bad things happen to good people? That is a question that has been around since the days of Cain and Abel. As long as God gives people agency to act for themselves they are free to inflict injustice on others. Likewise, they are free to do as much good as they can in the same world.

"May I ask you another question?" she asked somewhat sheepishly.

"Sure," I responded.

"You said that God loves me and that He is all powerful and that He is my Heavenly Father." I was nodding as she spoke. "Why did He let this happen to me?"

Now the difficult question was out in the open. I thought for a minute trying to measure my response with what I knew and what I believed. Here was a young woman whom I had recently taught to pray to and trust in a loving God. I found myself wondering to some degree why God would allow this to happen to a small child. Regardless of my own questions, she needed some reassurance about the One who knows all things.

"Dani," I began, "God does know everything. I know that if He allowed this to happen to you, He must have known you would be strong enough to get through this and He would provide a way for you to be healed in the process."

She looked up and gave me a feeble but trusting smile.

"And besides," I continued smiling, "He provided me to help you through it."

A question came into my mind. "Dani? Did these questions arise from some recent memories?"

She nodded and then looked down embarrassed.

"It is okay. Do you want to share those with me now?"

This time she shook her head.

"Can I send them in an email?" she asked as if she expected me to respond negatively.

"Of course, you can," I said. I was pleased that she was able to share these experiences with me even though they were embarrassing and horrible to her.

After our usual prayer, which she insisted I offer, she left our interview with an agreement to send these memories to me as soon as she could.

As I watched her leave I offered a prayer of thanks that this young woman was finally receiving some healing and that she was finding a way to have God once more in her life.

CHAPTER 9

Life Gets Worse

"To pray with faith means to pray expecting God to answer your prayers! Expect that they will be heard and He will come to your aid."
—From Dani's Diary

Dani had just experienced a really good day. She got to wear one of her pretty dresses to go to church. She got to sit next to her best friend in Primary, and she was even asked to stand in front of the whole group and hold a poster. In class, she learned about Jesus and prayer. She didn't realize she could pray to God or that God would even hear her. Such thoughts had never occurred to her. The teacher told the class that they should pray every morning and night and when they felt like they needed help.

That evening Dani decided to kneel beside her bed to pray. As she knelt there she tried to remember all that her teacher had said about what to do and the words to say. Had she heard the door to her bedroom open or sensed the figure standing there she would have been afraid.

The first hint she had that someone was there was when she felt a heavy blow from a well-placed kick which sent her sprawling across the carpet and into the dresser. With a look of shock and surprise she turned her eyes up and saw her father standing above her. What did she do wrong? Her mind raced yet she couldn't think of a thing she had done.

"So, you want to pray, do you?" He yelled at her as he landed another kick. Dani saw it coming and covered her face deflecting the blow. Her side and arms hurt horribly. Tears formed in her eyes. She knew if she cried out it would only be worse. Whatever she had done she knew it must have been her fault.

"I'm sorry," She tried to speak the words but it came out no louder than a hoarse whisper.

A large hand grabbed her by the hair and lifted her up so that her face was close to his. She saw anger in his eyes. There was something else, hate! This made her heart break. Why doesn't her father love her like he does the other kids?

"So, you want to pray? Understand this, you worthless piece of garbage, you don't pray without my permission. Do you understand?"

Before she could answer and without warning she felt a blow to her stomach. She let out a painful moan.

"Understand?" he asked again.

She quickly nodded.

"You only say the words I tell you to say, understand?"

She expected another hit but it didn't come. Slowly he released his grip on her hair, then as though in response to an afterthought he tightened his grip and lifted her up so that her little feet were an inch or two off the floor. She winced at the pain in her head and she saw stars until he dropped her beside the bed.

"From now on I will tell you the words to say in your prayers. You don't pray unless I tell you what to say. Understand?"

Another kick to her backside caused Dani's head to start nodding again.

"Your teacher lied to you. God doesn't exist, say it!" Not wanting to get another kick, she said it.

"I am your god!" he said. "You will pray to me. Say it!"

Dani repeated it again and again. After saying it repeatedly she lost count of the number of times she said those words. He gave the words to say in her prayers over and over again and she repeated them. She asked him to forgive her for being so wicked and evil. She asked him to help her to be obedient to him. She was told to say that even though she was a wicked girl and not lovable that she would do everything she was told. She was sorry she was hopeless and worthless. Dani lost track of the time. Every time she hesitated or appeared to fall asleep she received a whack on her head. She was sorry she had ever knelt down to pray.

Dani bounded through the door after school. The day had been an exciting one, full of interesting visitors and live creatures. One of those creatures, of all things, was a live snake. Just thinking about those eyes that didn't close and the tongue that darted in and out of its plastic-type mouth still gave her the shivers. She was recounting all the events of the day to her mother. The airplane pilot, the fireman, and the policeman were highlights. It was while she was telling her mom about policemen that her dad walked into the kitchen behind her. She continued telling how the policeman had told how if something was wrong you could always call a policeman for help. Then she heard the voice behind her.

"Dani," It was her father. His voice was more pleasant than usual. "Come here now!"

Obediently she turned on her heel and followed her father out of the kitchen. He grabbed her hair so tight it hurt as he dragged her down the hall and into her bedroom. She wondered what she had done wrong. She was always doing something wrong.

He sat on the bed while Dani stood in front of him. She was so confused. He seemed pleasant and almost nice. She almost thought that her dad had changed. Then with almost lightning speed his face changed to rage and he hit her in her stomach. She doubled over in pain. He grabbed her hair and pulled her upright.

"I am talking to you. It is very rude to look down when I am talking. Do you understand? Look at me!" He was yelling now.

Dani nodded through the pain and looked up.

"He lied to you," he said. "The policeman lied to you. He is not really there to help you."

Dani tried not to show surprise because she didn't want to anger him even more.

"You don't really know how they work. You don't ever want to talk to a policeman. You understand?" He punched her again in the stomach. "Do you!"

She nodded through the tears and said, "Yes."

"Do you know what they will do to you? Do you?"

She shook her head. She had no idea what he was talking about.

"If you go to a policeman he will see right through you. He will see how worthless and evil you are. He will know what kind of girl you really are. They will take you away from your family and put you in a dark room all by yourself. You will never be able to come back to your family again. Do you want that to happen? Do you?"

Dani just stood there trying to comprehend what she was being told. She remembered the nice man and his pleasant face. She couldn't believe that he would do that. But she also didn't want to be taken away from her family. She didn't want to live in a small dark room. It terrified her beyond her imagination.

"So, what do you do when you see a policeman?" he asked. His face was still masked in rage.

Dani said the only thing that came to her mind. Her response even made her dad smile.

"Run," she said. "Run."

Several weeks had passed since the moment that the memories started coming so quickly, increasing both in number and severity. We were both overwhelmed for a time. She now seemed to have settled into a routine of sending emails with these horrible memories and scenes. In return, I would read them and then make comments, sometimes within the text of her emails. I would explain how the abusive acts that had happened to her were wrong and that a loving father would not treat his daughter that way. I would reinforce the teachings of the Savior and the reality of a loving God who could heal any hurt or sorrow or pain. The most difficult part was trying to help her feel that she was not worthless and that God loves everyone: rich and poor, those in bondage and those who are free, even those who are abused.

After each memory or experience, Dani would express her belief that it happened because it was her fault. I would reassure her each time that it was not her fault. In this she found some comfort. I found it interesting that later she would not seem to remember our discussion concerning the concept of fault and I had to repeat and reinforce the truth that it was not her fault.

In spite of the nature of these memories and their impact emotionally on her, Dani appeared to be quite upbeat and cheerful. I had my job, she had hers, and working together seemed to be having a positive effect on her emotionally.

The events of her recent memories were disturbing. All possible avenues of help were being removed from Dani's childhood mind.

Several of her memories dealt with not trusting. The abuser sought to take away the two sources of help that any child would have the ability to turn to, policemen and God. By eliminating her ability to turn to either one, he had attempted to cut her off from even considering seeking help. This reminded me of the Elizabeth Smart kidnapping in Utah in 2002, while around the country we watched spellbound as the events unfolded. At one point, Elizabeth walked right down the city street in disguise with her kidnappers, but did not call out or run for help. Now I understood the reasons she may have kept silent. In spite of all of her father's efforts, however, Dani never quit believing in God. She even said an occasional prayer in her mind. This was remarkable to me. She never allowed her father, or anyone, to take complete control over her. In the face of all that was evil, she maintained a tiny belief in the Infinite.

During the early experiences with Dani, I came to believe that the abuse she had experienced happened in her long ago past. I surmised with relief that at least she was in no immediate danger. Unfortunately, I would soon find out that my thinking about her safety was seriously flawed.

Dani sat in the solitude of her bedroom for quite some time. She didn't know exactly how long she had been there. Hours? Days? Without a clock in her room it would have been impossible to know. Her dad had insisted that the windows be covered so that the room was mostly dark, nearly all the time.

She knew he was mad at her. She had gotten angry and had fought back. She knew it was a stupid idea to fight back. He was bigger and stronger and always won, but she didn't want to be hurt anymore. He always came in the middle of the night and surprised her. She tried hiding but there were few places to hide in the locked bedroom. He always found her. She tried to stay awake, she really tried. But he always came after she was asleep. Last night was different though. She had put her rubber soled shoes on, she stayed dressed and sat up on the edge of the bed leaning against the bed post. This way, when he came in, she would be ready.

In spite of the preparations she eventually dozed off. By the time she heard the lock turn and the creaking of the door it was too late. He grabbed her hair while at the same time she lashed out with her feet. The shoes connected with something, she thought probably a leg. She heard her dad give a muffled cry of both pain and surprise.

This only seemed to infuriate him. "So, you think you can fight me, do you? You will learn your place. You will learn you cannot fight me!" She struggled to fight back but he pinned her legs. She felt her shoes being removed and then her pants and shirt. She started to scream but before she could get it out she felt a powerful punch to her stomach. All the air that would have been there for a scream left and she found herself fighting for breath, any breath.

He stopped for a minute. It was quiet. All she could hear was something scraping across the floor. It was the bat. "No!" she thought. "Not again!" Dani knew what was going to happen. She tensed for it.

The beating seemed to last forever. She remembered little, except for some of his comments.

"You are a filthy waste of space."

"I should have discarded you when I had the chance."

"You will learn you cannot fight me. You will never win."

"I own you! There is nowhere you can go or hide. I will always find you and make you pay for it, understand?"

"You are only good for one thing."

Afterward she lay there in a heap, too exhausted and sore to move. She ached everywhere, even her bones felt like they ached from the repeated hits of the bat. She had known it was a mistake to fight back but she had to try. She just had to try.

In the hallway, she heard voices. Her mom and dad were fighting again. It always scared her when their voices got louder. However, she thought if she could just hear what they said, it might prepare her for the next beating or maybe even her mother would come to her rescue.

Her mom's voice had calmed down. "But I just can't understand it," her mom was almost pleading with her husband. "She used to be such a sweet girl!"

"Well, look for yourself what your sweet daughter did!" Her dad spat out the words.

Dani crawled across the floor to the door. Slowly, careful not to make a sound, she opened the door a crack to watch. As the sliver of light fell across her head her eyes adjusted to the change. She knew if her dad noticed her, she would be in a lot of trouble. In this moment, however, her curiosity overcame her fear. She watched as her dad showed her the bruise forming on his leg and the fingernail scratches on his arm. She didn't remember the scratches. It had all happened so fast.

"I just don't understand," she said again. Her voice was almost slurred when she spoke.

"I told you this would happen. It is all because you didn't listen to me. I think God is punishing you. You should have gotten rid of her when you had the chance. Now we are stuck with her!"

"Yes, but . . ." she buried her head in her hands, "I can't believe she has gone crazy."

"Probably runs in your side of the family," he said partially under his breath.

Her dad paused for a minute as if in thought and spoke again. His voice was suddenly calm and soothing.

"I know that this is distressing to you. I am sorry I said anything. Don't worry, I will take care of everything."

"What do you mean?"

"Obviously she is unstable. Something in her has snapped. I can't believe she attacked me either. So . . ." he paused as if reaching a decision, "I will be responsible for watching over her."

"But . . ."

"No buts. I didn't want to tell you but she said that you were wicked and evil and that she hated you."

"Really?"

"I know you didn't want to hear that. In her current condition, she might even hurt the children or even herself. I think it is best that she stay in her room until I come home from work. She will be by my side all the time. I will watch her so that she doesn't have one of her fits. That way she won't hurt you or the children."

"Why don't we take her to the doctor?"

"No!" he yelled and then lowered his voice. Dani had seen that quick response to anger before. "Do you want a scandal? Do you want people to find out what you did years ago? Think of your standing in the Ward. Remember how gossip spreads? Do you want that? Do you want to be ostracized? And think of the children; they will have to live with that shame and ridicule. No, it's not fair to them. I think this is for the best."

"Are you sure? Are you really sure?"

"Trust me. God has told me this is the best way to handle it. I will take care of everything. Now you go take a couple more sleeping pills and go back to bed. Don't worry about anything. You just try to feel better."

Slowly, with slumped shoulders, her mom disappeared down the hallway as Dani watched her through the door of her bedroom.

Dani observed her dad as he turned, smiled, and went down the stairs. She quietly closed the door. She knew it was going to be worse. Her mom would not be there to help her. Sore, aching from more places than she could count, Dani quietly sobbed in the dark corner of the room. Her sobbing had nothing to do with her pain. It had everything to do with her newfound hopelessness.

Some early memories seemed to indicate that Dani had experienced a fairly normal beginning. Family life was highlighted with family activities, trips, and playing with siblings. Sometime during first grade things seemed to change in family dynamics. Mom became sick and appeared to be on medications. Dad was working fulltime and also going to school and was probably experiencing stress and pressure. Dani's memories also revealed that the medications her mom was taking took her out of family life, sometimes for long periods of time. There were times when Dani tried to wake her mother, but the medicated sleep was too overwhelming for her mother to even notice her little girl. Her demeanor changed over time from a loving and sensitive mother to a harsh and mean overseer taking her anger and frustration out on Dani.

Her dad seemed to have manipulated the family to slowly remove Dani from normal family activities. This allowed him to have more and more control over the family. This transition appeared to be gradual. For one thing, he was telling the family how unstable Dani was. He painted the picture that she could be prone to violent episodes. He assured them that he would take care of it. Call a doctor? Out of the question. Embarrassment and reputation were at stake. Who wants other church members and neighbors to think that their family had a crazy person who could be potentially dangerous? They would be shunned and it wouldn't be fair for the other children in the family. The children adopted the subtle lies and eventually Dani was no longer considered one of the children. She became almost invisible. Her father's arguments had been compelling and logical. It would have to be a family secret. No one could know the truth. They must have all eventually agreed for the good of the family.

Several questions remained unanswered. Why was the secret created in the first place? Was it to hide his abuse and to keep anyone from finding out the truth? And why the abuse in the first place? Why was Dani the focus of the repeated abuse? The other children appeared to have a relatively normal relationship with Mom and Dad. What would cause a father to focus his abuse on one child? Resentment? Jealousy? My mind pondered over these questions. I just didn't have enough information to find definite answers and maybe never would. Still, I HAD to find some answers for Dani's sake.

Dani started to feel like she was being crushed by a huge mountain of guilt. She felt that everything was her fault. I was beginning to understand why she felt that way. With each new limitation of her freedom she was told it was her fault. She never knew the reason why nor was she given any explanation.

For most families, one of the focal points of each day is the dinner table. It is a time where families get one good meal a day together. Parents and children discuss the activities of the day and lessons can be taught regarding manners and rules. Very health-conscious parents ensure that their children eat nutritious and balanced meals. Dani's early life was very similar and she enjoyed eating with the whole family. When the changes occurred, she found that she had to now sit next to her father at each meal. He started berating her in front of the other children saying she was fat and didn't deserve to eat. Over time her father started to limit what and how much she could eat. She remembered finally that she was allowed to have only one item on her plate. As she ate her meager portion, she was instructed that her situation was her own fault. If she wasn't so fat or stupid or disobedient or some other belittlement, she would get more food. All of this would go on while the rest of the family continued to act in normal ways with children eating what they wanted and even asking for dessert while Dani ate her restricted diet.

Dani was constantly wondering what she was doing wrong and why the other children didn't receive the same treatment. She thought if she would just try harder, be more obedient or nicer, her dad would return to the way he was before. She did her best, but it didn't seem to matter. Dani tried hard to be obedient and listen to her father but it didn't seem to lessen her father's anger toward her. Sometimes just the very sight of her could kindle his rage. No matter what she did to try to make him happy, nothing dampened the flow of his abusiveness toward her. Eventually her siblings started to avoid her and bought into the fabrication that she was somehow insane and would not even engage in conversation with their sister.

After one of our sessions, Dani left my office and made her way to the entrance of the church. It was dusk, everyone had gone home leaving Dani and I alone inside the church building. Because appointments were set at different times, the church was not locked until I left at the end of the day.

I had an afterthought regarding our interview. I decided to try to catch Dani before she drove off. As I exited the building I saw something that made my blood run cold. Across the parking lot next to Dani's car was a man who appeared to be having a discussion with Dani. He was tapping his finger on her chest and I could tell the words he was using were direct and angry.

"Dani?" I called. "Are you okay?"

I said the words as I was walking across the parking lot to intervene.

Without turning to see who was coming, the man said one last word, turned, and walked quickly to the end of the parking lot and disappeared around the fence.

"Are you okay?" I asked again as I came up beside her.

"Yes," she replied but I could tell she was afraid.

"Do you know who that was?"

She paused before answering.

"No, I don't," she finally replied. "I need to go home now."

Without another word, she got into her car and drove off in the direction of her home.

I had an uneasy feeling that she indeed did know this person. It was obvious that he was surprised that I had come out of the church and interrupted what he was doing. Dani was definitely afraid of him.

I made myself two new rules. First, lock up the church during our interviews. Second, at the end of each session I would walk Dani safely to her car.

CHAPTER 10

Life in a Closet

Once long ago before my birth, I learned that I must prepare to face the trials here on earth and rely on my Father's care, and in the darkest hours of life, when it feels as if no one is there, I will not fear when I am safe in my Father's care.
—FROM THE SONG *MY FATHER'S CARE* (OLSEN, 1992)

The covers were warm and comfortable. Dani had not felt this secure for a long time. She felt something shaking her. In the fogginess between sleep and consciousness, she thought it was a cute little puppy tugging and pulling on the blanket. She smiled at the thought of it. She tried to reach out to feel the thick soft fur. Then the puppy seemed to grow within seconds to a large viscous dog who was pouncing on her back repeatedly, jumping harder and harder. As she turned to get away from the dog her eyes opened and she realized it was a dream. The haze cleared and the large dog turned into her mother.

"Get out of bed, you little brat. Now!" her mom shouted.

Dani stumbled from the bed and rolled on the floor and into the wall. She ended up sitting cross legged on the floor with her back against the wall. Instinctively her hands went up to protect her from the anticipated blow. It didn't come immediately.

"You're being punished," she continued. Her mother started opening the dresser drawers and throwing clothes on the floor just outside the door.

"Why?" Dani asked.

"Bad girls don't deserve to have things. They don't get the privileges the good kids get."

Dani didn't understand what her mother was saying. What did she do that was bad? Why was her mother taking away her things? Why didn't her mother love her? These were questions that didn't have any answers for her.

Her mother finished with the chest of drawers and moved to the closet. All the while she was yelling at Dani. Her dresses and shoes were next as she watched them thrown out the door.

"You are a wicked little girl! Why couldn't you have died? You have ruined everything."

Dani's little mind was racing. She heard what was being said, but didn't fully understand. How could she have ruined everything? And what did her mother mean that she should have died? In frustration Dani started to cry. Her mother stopped what she was doing and smacked her across her head.

"Stop being a baby!" she said. "It is all your fault anyway." In a state of overwhelm and lack of comprehension Dani began to sob.

Her mother hit her on the head a couple of times. "You have no right to cry. It's your fault anyway. If you want any of these things back, you will have to earn them. Stop it!" she yelled. Dani stifled her sobbing.

Next went her toys. Her mother scooped them up in her arms and tossed them on top of the other items.

"Now your clothes."

Dani looked uncomprehendingly at her mother.

"Now!" came the demand.

Dani removed her clothes until she stood there in the room in just her panties. Her mother took the rest of the clothes and threw them out of the room as well.

"Into the closet." Her mother held the door handle in one hand and pointed with the other. Slowly, Dani stood up and moved toward the closet.

"If you don't want me to have your dad punish you, you had better not come out of the closet until I let you out. Understand?"

Dani meekly nodded. She entered the empty closet and turning, she sat on the floor. Her mother slowly disappeared as the closet door closed and left her alone in the dark. Only a sliver of light emanated from the crack at the bottom of the door. The world around her became one of lonesome darkness.

"I am being followed." I received a text on my phone. I knew it was from Dani. I pulled my car over on a quiet street. I was in the middle of my workday and about forty minutes from home. I quickly dialed her number.

"What do you mean you are being followed?" I asked.

She hadn't communicated with me for several days.

"A car started following me when I left the house," she responded in a matter-of-fact way.

"Did you see who is following you?" I felt the adrenalin kicking in.

"Yeah. That car has been sitting out in front of the house off and on for the past two days."

"Do you recognize the car?"

Dani's voice sounded calm but there was an edge of worry to it. "I don't know. I think it might be my dad. The car looks kinda familiar." There was a long pause and then she said, "What do I do? I am scared."

"Who do you have in the car with you?"

"Just my two girls," she replied.

"Can you tell me where you are right now?" I asked quickly. My concern was not only for her safety but also for the kids. I had no idea what the car's driver might be capable of doing to them. This whole situation could be nothing or it could turn into something tragic. I decided it was better to err on the side of caution.

"Maybe I should stop. If it is my dad he would be mad if I didn't. It is probably all my fault anyway."

"Dani, please listen to me. What you are saying are the memories speaking. It is not true. It wasn't your fault. It never was. IT WAS NEVER YOUR FAULT." I added the last part with emphasis to make a point and to punch through the control the memories were having on her.

"Really? Because it feels like it is my fault."

"You need to believe me, Dani. It is not your fault. You were a little girl. Think of your little girls. How could something like that be their fault?"

Several seconds passed without a sound. My heart was racing because I didn't know how she would react. My fear was that she might revert back to the abused little girl and stop, or even worse, allow herself to be abused once more.

"Dani, do you trust me?" I asked.

"Yes," she said. "Please tell me what to do?" She gave me the name of the street she was on. I was very familiar with that area.

"The police station is only three blocks from there, can you get there okay?" I commented.

"No!" she exclaimed. "I don't want to go there. They scare me."

"But I don't think he will follow you there. I am pretty sure he doesn't want to make a scene."

"No!" she was emphatic this time. My mind raced for an alternative solution.

"Then, I want you to drive to Costco. Don't stop and don't get out of the car if he is still following."

"Why?" she asked.

"Because there are a lot of people there. My guess is that he will not want to approach you unless he can be assured that he can get you alone. I think that he will quit following you." It all made sense to me. I reasoned that she would be safer in a crowd than in an empty parking lot. I was already silently praying for God's help.

"I'll do what you are telling me."

"Call me and let me know how it went, okay?"

"I will," she replied.

"And whatever you do, keep the doors locked and do not get out of the car if you see that car near you." At that point, the line went dead. Uncertain about my promptings, I wondered if I had given her safe and sound advice.

How long she had been in the closet she did not know. It could have been for hours. She had fallen asleep and awakened only to find pitch blackness. She experienced a sudden twinge of fear. It occurred to her that there were no sounds: no voices, no music, no laughter, nothing to indicate that anyone was home. She felt all alone. She craved her mother's touch and to be held in her arms once more, to be told she was loved and wonderful. How she longed to feel safe and protected and to be told everything would be alright. She had no idea why she was being punished. What had she done? Why was she still in the closet?

It was then she felt the emptiness in her stomach. She couldn't remember the last time she had eaten. She was not only hungry but she had an undeniable thirst as well. It was at this point that overwhelm set in. She started to sob.

As time dragged on she could hear the creaks and groans of the home, expanding and contracting with the change in temperature. She could even hear the beat of her own heart. Paramount on her mind now was the overwhelming need to use the bathroom. She called out for her mom and dad.

"I have to go to the bathroom."

She yelled out several times but her shouts went unanswered. She dared not leave because she knew she would be severely punished. She waited and waited as long as she could when finally, she could not hold it any longer and she felt the warmth of her urine soaking her underwear and puddling on the surrounding floor beneath her. She began to sob once more. This time it was out of humiliation and embarrassment. She was beginning to think this night would never end.

The longer the day went on the more worried I became. Since she had told me about being followed I couldn't help but imagine the worst. Although Dani was becoming more and more self-confident, I knew she was still very vulnerable and would crumble under the type of domineering control her dad appeared to be capable of.

As if in response to my thoughts my cell phone rang and I was relieved to see it was Dani on the caller ID. Some of my anxiety let itself go.

"Hello, Dani," I answered eagerly. "Are you still being followed?"

"No," she replied. "I am home now."

"Are you okay? What happened?"

"I did what you said," she reported. "And they quit following. So, I drove around for quite a while to make sure I wasn't being followed, then, I drove home. Thank you for your help."

"You are welcome."

I felt a great sense of relief but there was still worry in her voice. After a longer than normal pause she spoke.

"Someone has been in my house." Although she said it without much emotion, I could tell she was afraid.

"How do you know?" I asked.

"Things are thrown around."

"What kind of things?" I felt like I was pulling information out of her. She may have been in shock. I suppressed my need to have answers and chose to remain quiet.

"That is the odd thing. Only my things were touched. The kid's things, Jeff's things were left alone. Someone went through my things in the bathroom and in my closet and drawers. Mostly my underwear was tossed around the room."

"Your underwear?" I asked in surprise.

"Yes. I feel embarrassed. I am sorry."

"Don't be sorry," I tried to comfort her. "It's going to be okay."

"I don't feel safe anymore. This was the only place besides your office that I have felt safe. Not even this place is safe anymore."

"Dani, I think we should call the police," I replied. "They can investigate and find out who . . ."

"No!" Dani cut me off in midstream. "I can't call the police. I can't. They won't understand." She was firm and resolute. Conceding this idea, I opted for another approach.

"How did they get in?"

"That's just it," she replied with a puzzled inflection. "I don't know."

"Okay, Dani, I would like you to hang up right now. Check every door and every window. See which ones were unlocked or broken or open. That will let us know. When you are finished, call me back. Understand?"

"I understand," she replied and I heard a click ending the call.

Dani awoke to a horrid acrid smell. The confined space of the closet and the lack of ventilation magnified the odor. The line of light at the bottom of the closet door brought a shimmer of hope to her heart as daylight had come. There were no clues to indicate how long she had been in the confined space. She had lost all track of time, long enough that she no longer had a desire to go to the bathroom. She was sitting on the only spot on the floor that hadn't been soiled during her long incarceration.

Her thirst was now overpowering. She licked her lips to find the skin broken and bleeding. She felt weak and more tired than usual.

She said a silent prayer. As she prayed she could hear her heart beating and found herself asking God to stop her heart so she could go to heaven. As she prayed, she told God that if heaven was not possible that anywhere that was safe would be okay. But mostly she wanted to die, to end it, so it would be over. As she ended her prayer she began to sob once more.

Suddenly the closet door opened flooding the little space with light. It was so bright Dani had to raise her arm to cover her eyes against sunlight from the bedroom window. Silhouetted in the light was her father. She felt a shudder of fear ripple through her.

"Why are you so loud?" He was angry. He always seemed to be angry she thought. "Why are you being such a little baby? You had better be quiet and now! You are interrupting my family."

She was slowly trying to process what he said. She was not part of the family? What did he mean? She tried to say 'sorry' but the word couldn't get past her lips.

"Look at you!" He grabbed her arm and yanked her out of the closet so that she was standing on wobbly legs against the wall next to the door.

She felt his penetrating gaze, judging and searching, which magnified her embarrassment. "You are filthy and dirty. Look what you have done." He gestured to the soiled closet floor. "You are no better than the mess on the floor. Hear me?" He was yelling as she feebly nodded.

She wanted to explain that it wasn't her fault, that she had called for help and no one came but she thought better of it.

"You are garbage. You understand me?" Dani looked down and nodded.

"Well? What do you want?"

She was afraid to ask but the need was just too great. "Water? Please?" the response was hoarse and through cracked lips. Without saying anything he turned on his heel and left the room. After a couple of minutes, he returned with a glass of water and set it on the floor.

"Is that what you want?" he asked. But before she could answer he punched her in the stomach. She doubled over in pain.

"Is that what you want? Is it?" his voice was taunting her now.

"Tell me!" he yelled.

Dani tried to straighten her slight frame.

"Yes, please." Her reply was almost a whisper.

He started laughing at her. "Look at you! You are dirty and worthless and dripping with sh**! Why would anyone want you or love you?" He hit her again.

"You are the biggest mistake I have ever made!" Another blow landed. She heard him through the haze and pain. "I should not have listened to your mom." He hit her again. This time she fell to her knees and then to the floor. "I should have shut her up before I ended up with you!"

Dani felt another hit and then another. All the while he was laughing at her, calling her fat, trash, and garbage. Finally, when the beating was over she was exhausted and could barely move. She lay in a fetal position as he rolled her with his feet until she was back in the closet looking out. As the door closed, Dani watched the glass of water with longing until she was plunged into darkness again.

"Everything looks fine." Dani had called back after more than twenty minutes went by. She was slightly winded. "Sorry. The kids needed a snack. That's why it took so long."

"So, no broken or unlocked windows," I asked.

"None broken. All were securely closed."

I was completely stumped. I was sure that she would find an open window where any criminal would find easy entry. My mind started racing to figure out what it could be. I tried to think of ways for someone to enter a house without forcing their way in. If there was no forced entry then whoever came in had to have a key or something. I thought about my own house and then an idea came to me.

"Dani, do you have a door to the garage from the inside?"

She replied after a brief pause. "Yes. It is just off the kitchen. We leave it unlocked. But the garage door is closed and Jeff said it is safe."

"Ordinarily that is true because you have to have a remote garage door opener to open the door. How many openers do you have?"

She thought for a minute before she replied. "We have only one now," she replied.

"What do you mean NOW?" I asked. "Were there more?"

"We had two but one went missing a couple of weeks ago. We just figured one of the kids lost it."

"That has to be it!" My excitement was increasing as we were approaching a possible solution. "Did you have any visitors or unusual experiences in the past couple of weeks?"

Again, I was greeted with silence on the other end of the line. I just assumed that she was thinking.

After a while I asked, "Dani, are you alright?"

After a long minute, she replied with a sheepish tone. "Are you going to be mad at me?"

"I won't be mad at you," I replied patiently. "What happened?"

Hesitantly she told me how she was expecting a friend to stop by. So, when there was a knock on the door her mom and dad were there and pushed their way past her into the house. Her dad yelled at her for not answering their phone calls and cutting them off. Her mom was in the process of taking the kids into the back room as her dad grabbed her arm and roughly pulled her up the stairs. At that moment Jeff happened to come home from work early and came in the door as she was being pulled up the stairs towards the bedrooms. After he asked what was going on, her mom and dad instantly became all smiles and congeniality and explained that they had missed the grandchildren and their daughter and had just come by to spend some time with them. Then as quickly as they had come, they left. Jeff found it odd that they had just got there and now didn't want to see their grandchildren. Dani was just relieved that they had left and she had almost forgotten the incident.

"I didn't say anything because I thought you'd be mad at me," she said as she concluded retelling the occurrence.

"Dani, there is no way I'd be mad at you. I just worry for your safety. Why did you think I'd be mad? "

"Everybody gets mad at me. I just thought you'd be the same."

My heart ached to think that this was what Dani expected from those around her. I have seen parents doing the opposite, going overboard with their children, telling them in glowing terms how wonderful they were, and making them feel more than special. What a contrast to the horrible expectation Dani had of everyone in her life to exact their worst on her.

"I think we can make your home safe again. My guess is that when your dad was in the house, he took one of the garage openers and that is how he is getting into the house. That would explain no forced entry and why only your things were disturbed. I think he was giving you a message that he can get to you any time he wants. But we are going to fool him. Do you like that idea?"

She readily agreed. I then instructed her how she could make her home safe again. I told her to start locking the door between the house and the garage. As an added precaution, I suggested that she enable the 'lock' button on the inside control by the door. That way the remote would not work from the outside until the 'lock' button was turned off. Satisfied that she was safe once more within her own house, I made one more suggestion.

"While Jeff is changing the remote code and getting a new remote for you, have him pick up a peephole for the front door. This will allow you to see who is there before opening the door."

Surprisingly, she had never heard of a peephole, but she was sure Jeff could find it and get it installed for her.

"And Dani?"

"Yes?" she replied.

"I am glad you're safe."

"Me too," she replied. "Me too. And . . . thank you."

The current memories that Dani was experiencing were taking their toll emotionally on her. She was having a difficult time reconciling the actions of her parents with her limited recollection of her childhood. She just couldn't believe they could have treated her that way, and she constantly wondered what could possibly be wrong with her that would cause them to be so cruel to her. In each of our discussions she consistently took upon herself all of the blame for her parents' actions. She would always indicate that the abuse must have been because of something she had done. I never once heard her put blame on her parents, and amazingly she never expressed anger or hatred toward them. The only consistent emotion expressed was fear. She just didn't want to be hurt again.

Betrayal was also on her mind constantly. She was not concerned about being betrayed by her parents but she felt that she was betraying them. She was afraid that by telling me her memories, she was betraying them. I had to constantly remind her that she was the one being abused. Normal and reasonable parents didn't treat their children this way. She had a difficult time with the concept. I could only assume that her reaction was the result of the abuse and consistent brainwashing.

It was also surprising that when Dani started sharing these very difficult memories, the pressure appeared to be increasing daily with cars following her, abusive phone calls, and attempts to invade her home. The world itself was trying to stop Dani from sharing her past with someone. I found it unusual that both would be happening at the same time.

Shortly after making the suggestion about the peephole, I received a call from Dani indicating that Jeff didn't know the first thing about installing the new security device. I made one phone call to a member of our congregation who was a handyman, and within 24 hours it was installed. As I drove by I had to smile. The handyman had even installed it lower, making it convenient for Dani's short height to easily see through it. The only thing that could make her home safer, I mused, would be security cameras around the house.

CHAPTER 11

Throwaway Child

Being unwanted, unloved, uncared for, forgotten by everybody - I think that is a much greater hunger, a much greater poverty than the person who has nothing to eat.
—Mother Teresa

She ached. The pain throbbed through her little body. She remembered that she was seven years old. She had just been beaten. She was sore and bleeding. Then she heard something comforting. It was a song and it was filtering through the house. Even in the small cramped space in the closet she could make out the lyrics. The song penetrated the locked door as well as the darkness and entered into her soul. She could just barely make out the words.

Abide with me; 'tis eventide,
The day is past and gone;
The shadows of the evening fall;
The night is coming on.
Within my heart a welcome guest,
Within my home abide.
O Savior, stay this night with me;
Behold, 'tis eventide,
O Savior, stay this night with me;
Behold, 'tis eventide.
(by Harrison Millard, *Hymns*, 1985)

It must have been coming from her dad's bedroom. The song was so sweet and touching. Something inside her stirred. She couldn't help it, she started to cry.

Then she heard footsteps coming quickly. She knew it was her dad. She heard the lock turn on the bedroom door and the closet door swung open.

"What the hell are you doing? What are you crying about?" He was angry again.

"Could I please just hear more of that song?" Something about the song gave her strength and courage. It comforted her and made her almost feel loved.

Her answer was a kick. He grabbed her hair and dragged her out of the closet. Another kick, and another.

"This song is not meant for someone like you!" Those words stung. Not meant for her?

"God hates you. You are worthless, throwaway garbage. God threw you away, he doesn't want you."

Then the beating started over again.

"God hates you, say it!" he yelled.

"God hates me." she replied back.

"God hates you, say it!" He kept yelling.

She kept repeating. She lost track of how many times she was forced to say it.

After a while the song lost its meaning. The part where it touched her heart faded. After what seemed like hours of beating and kicking, she laid crumpled again in the dark closet. At least the darkness was friendly. She hurt so badly. She laid there, energy spent and no will to fight back. Now there were no sounds, no music, only quiet. She eventually dozed off to a fitful sleep.

Life in the closet had become Dani's new normal. Life in the closet meant being hungry, thirsty and the most difficult . . . being alone.

As I reviewed with Dani some of the memories, I could tell they continued to take an emotional toll on her. Remembering the long hours of isolation caused her to wonder once more what she had done to deserve this treatment. Why her? What had she done? Why had she been punished? These were all questions that she asked and unfortunately there just weren't any answers. However, the solitude had allowed her to think of better times, playing in the yard, having snowball fights, and a prior family vacation. Oddly though, she found the experience in the closet gave her a feeling of safety and security. Most of the time there was no yelling or beatings.

"Promise you won't laugh at me?" Dani had gotten somewhat comfortable with asking questions. I guess she felt that with some of the things she had shared with me I was 'safe', as she termed it.

"I promise," I responded.

"I really got used to the closet. I don't know just how long I was kept there but it was a long time."

She shifted in her chair indicating that she was either uncomfortable or embarrassed.

"I remember that they would let me out of the closet in the morning. I put on my dress, got a few crusts of bread usually for breakfast, and went to school. I got so that I would open the closed door slightly and use the light in the room to do my homework."

"You did your homework in the closet?" I asked with a shocked expression.

"Oh, yes. I worked on it until I couldn't see any more and then I would sleep"

This response gave me some insight as to the amazing personality that was Dani. How many children in similar circumstances would be concerned enough to complete assigned homework on their own?

She continued her story.

"I had to wear the same dress every day. I remember that it was dirty and wrinkled. But at least I was not just in my underwear. And there was another benefit."

"What was that, Dani?" I asked.

"At school, I felt safe." She looked up and smiled weakly. "At school there were no beatings, no yelling, and no closet."

"So why didn't you tell anyone at school what was going on?" I asked.

"Because there are rules," she replied.

I remembered she had mentioned that once before. "Rules?" I asked, "What rules?" This seemed to be one of the keys her father had in controlling her.

"I can't tell you," she said.

"Oh, you can't remember them?" I ventured trying to draw responses out.

"No, I remember them just fine. I remember every single one of them. But I can't tell you. Maybe some time I can, but I am not ready. Not now."

"That's okay," I replied. "Whenever you are ready. So, tell me more."

"During that time, I was always kept separated from my brothers and sisters. I wasn't allowed to play with them or even be a part of their family nights. When I got home from school I was expected to go right to my room, take off the dress and go right into the closet. It was the same with church. At church, my dad would not let me out of his sight. He would make me sit with him all the time. Most of the time he would leave church early and take me home. And always back to the closet. So, you can see, it was my safe place."

"Did you miss not playing with your brothers or sisters or family activities?" I asked.

"Of course, I did. I ached to be just like other kids. I longed to just be held by my mother and fall asleep in her arms. I missed having my father treat me like he did the other kids. I feel like I lost my childhood."

"At least you're able to give your children a good childhood," I responded trying to be comforting.

She looked at me with a longing in her eyes; someone had stolen something most precious and prized and she was mourning its loss.

She was standing in the middle of the kitchen. Through the door children could be seen playing in the yard. Birds were singing in the trees as they chirped angry warnings to the trespassers below. A slight cooling breeze blew through the open window causing goosebumps to rise on her arms and back. Dani folded her arms to try to generate some warmth. She was standing in the middle of the kitchen in only her underwear. This was the only thing she had worn for weeks. Meager portions of food and water had sustained her in her solitary home in the closet. She seldom had visitors unless it was for a beating.

She was always told it was her fault. It was usually her father who came with some water or crusts of bread. The unusual visit had been her mother. About twenty minutes before she found herself in the kitchen, the door to the closet opened to reveal her mother standing there. Her heart skipped a beat and for a moment she thought her mom had come to rescue her. Her hopes spiraled downward as her mother spoke.

"What do you want?" she demanded.

"Just a little food please." Dani could have eaten much more but she only dared ask for a little.

Without a word, her mother grabbed her arm and dragged her down the stairs and into the kitchen. There she stood looking around while her mother sat the table and read a magazine. She saw the remnants of the family dinner on the table and stacked dirty dishes in the sink. She could smell the potatoes and fried chicken; her stomach took a leap. She wanted to run and grab it and shove it into her mouth but she knew better.

After what seemed forever her mother put down the magazine and looked at her. Dani longed for kind and loving eyes, but she only looked at Dani with disgust. Her mother stood in front of her with a plate of leftover food taken from the counter.

"Is this what you want?" she demanded. With that she grabbed a handful of mashed potatoes and shoved it into Dani's face.

"You don't even deserve this much!"

She could feel the food in her nostrils and in her eyes. She wanted to cry but summoned up what strength she had left to maintain her composure. As if in a dream, in slow motion she watched as the plate slowly left her mother's fingers and tumbled end over end until it crashed on the floor depositing food at Dani's feet.

"You are disgusting!" commented her mother shaking her head as she saw Dani eying the food on the floor.

Without hesitation Dani dropped to her knees and started grabbing handfuls of food and filling her mouth as fast as possible. She wanted to consume all she could before her mother stopped her. She didn't care that the food was on the floor or that the floor was dirty. When the food was gone she bent down and licked the floor until all the food was gone.

Remembering that her mother was still in the room, she glanced up and saw her mother looking away with disgust. Although hurt by her look, Dani found that she was grateful for the food. She silently muttered a brief prayer of thanks for the first food in days.

As if her mother could guess her thoughts Dani noticed that the look of disgust suddenly changed to anger. She felt her hair being yanked as her mother started yelling at her. She shouted hurtful, disgusting, and demeaning things. Then Dani watched as her gaze went from her to the corner of the kitchen and back to her. Dani noticed her dad's bat standing there. As her mom went to retrieve the bat Dani rushed to crawl under the table. When the first blow landed she had curled in a fetal position. The chair and table legs absorbed most of the force from the blows. Frustrated, her mother dropped the bat and left the kitchen. Before her mother could change her mind, Dani raced to the safety of the closet.

"I'm scared," Dani's voice sounded as if she were in an echo chamber through the phone.

My illuminated watch indicated 1:00 a.m. I was trying to shake the cobwebs of deep slumber out of my head. Picking up my vibrating phone I silently left the bedroom careful not to wake my wife.

"What's going on Dani?" I was finally alert.

"Someone is outside." Her voice was barely discernible; however, the fright and terror was obvious.

"Dani, can you speak louder?"

"No. I am afraid they will hear me."

I could detect an echo over the phone as she talked. It didn't sound normal. "Where are you?"

"I am sitting here in my closet with my kids."

"What?" I was incredulous. "Why are you in the closet?"

"They are pounding on the door." She was whispering still as though whoever it was could hear her on the second floor of her home tucked away in a closet.

"Who is it?" I asked emphatically. "Who is at the door?"

"I don't know. But it has to be him." she responded. "I know he is angry with me. I just know it. He wants me back."

I had a visual image of Dani and her children in the closet being terrorized by a person or persons unknown. Even in my tired state, I was becoming angry. No one should have to experience what she was going through.

"Dani, listen to me," I replied with authority. "You have to call the police."

"I can't!" she sounded even more frightened. "I just can't."

"Why? I think it is for the best."

"I just remembered something tonight. I want to tell you. I really do, but I am scared. Can I tell you later? Please?" The emphasis on the 'please' was a cross between fear and pleading.

"Now he is pounding on the back door. I am afraid he is going to get in."

"Where is Jeff?" I wondered why he wasn't there helping, protecting his family.

"He took his meds tonight. They always make him sleep. I couldn't wake him. I tried."

I knew there was only one thing I could do. "Dani? I am heading over to your house. I will be there in about five minutes. Okay? Just stay where you are and wait for my call."

A light rain was falling as I drove to Dani's house. It was that annoying type of rain where you can't decide whether it is better to have your wipers on or off. There were no cars on the road which wasn't surprising given the early morning hour. I purposely drove around the block so I could approach her home from the south. This way I could get a view of the back side of the house first and catch whoever it was in the act of pounding on the doors. I had no idea what to expect. I knew my anger level, along with some very excited adrenalin, had me in a high state of alertness and agitation.

As I approached the home I engaged my high beams flooding the rear of the house with light. With no fence or obstructions in the back yard everything was visible even in the rain. There would be no place to hide. Relief and disappointment came over me as my headlights revealed only a quiet and peaceful back yard. No shadowy images, no fleeing culprits. I drove around to the front of the house and allowed my high beams to wash over the front door and garage doors. Again, nothing.

I called Dani and informed her that there was nobody lurking around the outside of her home. She sounded genuinely surprised. I assured her that things were safe and they could all go back to bed.

I decided to do a perimeter search for broken windows or anything that might be amiss. I parked the car and turned off the engine while grabbing my flashlight. Exiting the car, I began my search. I found all doors secure and all windows locked. Nothing was broken or damaged. In fact, I started questioning why I was there at all; there was nothing at all out of place. There didn't seem to be any evidence that anyone had been out there. I half wished there had been some snow instead of rain because at least I could see any visible footprints.

I was starting to think I had been duped by a very overactive imagination. Was she imagining the sounds or experiencing a prior memory? Was she experiencing delusions? Just when I was about to give up and go home I saw it. Below a back window were fresh footprints in the mud. There was a spot where someone had slipped and put their hand down to steady their balance. Then what I saw made a shiver run down my spine. On the window were mud streaks, remnants of a failed attempt to push a window open. I hurriedly swung my beam of light in all directions around me. There was no sign of anyone. I didn't know whether to be disappointed or relieved.

Now fully awake and more adrenalin pumping, I knew I would not be able to get back to sleep anytime soon.

Sitting in her closet, Dani was trying to make a decision. She was driven by two strong emotions: fear and hunger. Her body screamed for food but she also knew that if she were caught that she would pay and pay dearly. Dani purposely waited until long past the last sounds of the family going to bed. She knew the house would be dark and she would have to be silent as a mouse for her plan to work.

Finally hunger won out and she slowly opened the bedroom door. Making sure that nobody was moving about and all was quiet, she made her way quietly down the hallway to the kitchen and into the pantry. She didn't dare turn on a light but left the pantry door open to allow the night light from the kitchen windows to illuminate the pantry. She grabbed the first thing she saw, a box of cereal. Without hesitation, she plunged her hand into the box and pulled out a fistful of cereal and shoved it into her mouth. After the third handful, she was startled by the bright light of the kitchen and she knew she had been caught. Her mother was not happy at all.

Dragging Dani by the hair she was led to the bathroom and told to stand by the wall near the toilet.

"So, you think you can steal food, do you?" her mother spat out. "Did you get enough?" Now she was taunting her.

Dani could see that she was rummaging through the medicine cabinet. Finally, her hand rested on a glass bottle with clear liquid in it. Dani could only see the word *Ipecac* on the label. Her mother twisted off the cap and handed it to Dani.

"Drink that," she demanded. "You will find out what happens to bad girls."

Dani was hesitant at first but seeing the resolve in her mother's eyes she lifted the bottle to her lips and took a swallow. Then she reached out to hand it back to her mother.

"Drink the whole damn thing," she commanded.

She thought about arguing with her, but knew better. She had taken food without permission. She had been so hungry. Hesitantly she finished the thick clear liquid and handed the empty bottle to her mother.

It didn't take long and she had the most horrible stomach cramps. She dove for the toilet and started throwing up. She threw up all the food she had eaten and yet her stomach kept cramping and causing her to gag. The spasms continued but nothing came from her empty stomach for the next several minutes.

"Now maybe you will learn your lesson," her mother sneered. "If you do this again you will get worse, understand?"

Dani nodded wiping spittle from her mouth with the back of her hand. Seeing her opportunity to leave, she scuttled back to the closet and waited while the cramping subsided. She had learned her lesson, one she knew she would never try to repeat.

Over the next few weeks the pounding continued. It was never at the same time or on consecutive days. Each time it happened it woke up the kids and they would huddle together once more in the closet afraid that whoever it was would break in and hurt them. Several times I parked down the street from the house with my lights off and partially hidden from view. I had watched enough 'Who-Done-It' shows to give me confidence that I knew what I was doing. I watched the house until the early morning hours and never saw a soul. It was as though whoever it was tormenting Dani's family somehow knew I was there. My attempts to catch someone in the act of this terrorism went unrewarded.

I spoke with Dani a few days after my last stakeout. I was trying to come up with solutions for this little family. In my mind, I could see the fresh footprints in the mud outside the house window and I knew the threat was real and that thought made my blood boil.

"I am sorry, Dani." I apologized.

"Why are you sorry?" she replied quizzically over the phone.

"I was hoping to catch them in the act, take a picture of them or something. But I just haven't been able to catch anyone outside your house."

"Thank you for everything," she replied with sincere gratitude. "It just doesn't seem fair! I am not angry or hate anyone. I just want to be left alone." She sounded very frustrated and almost resigned to the fact that this was the way life was supposed to be.

I really felt bad for her and her family. It was hard enough having three small children but she was also dealing with the reawakening of these past memories. The pain and emotions of each abusive memory would exhaust her emotionally and physically, sending her backwards on the road to wholeness. It required me to assist her in understanding those memories and rebuilding her self-worth. After working through each memory, I was able to show her how to reach out, time and time again, for the peace and love given freely through the Lord Jesus Christ.

Dani had come from a situation where she had been forced and taught not to pray. Additionally, she had been told that God didn't exist, and even if God did exist, He wouldn't want to from hear her anyway. It was quite possible that these teachings had literally been beaten into her.

She had now accepted that God was real and that there was an infinite atonement providing healing from all the abuse she had suffered. Embracing these teachings had begun to bring healing into her life along with much needed peace. I knew that these teachings would be challenged again and again before we would reach the end of her memories.

And now, in addition to all of her struggles, she was being terrorized. It was as though the devil himself was seeing the progress we were making and decided to take personal interest in destroying our work. Why would all this evil seem to focus on one young mom who just wanted to be left alone?

"It is really too bad," I said, half listening, while ideas hatched in my head: some very simple in nature, and some extreme like surrounding the house with a patrol of infantry soldiers. How I could accomplish that I did not know.

"What do you mean?" came Dani's reply.

I realized that I had been speaking out loud.

"Uh, hmmm, I was just thinking that if you guys just had a couple of security cameras outside your house, you could catch them in the act. But not the wireless type because I think they can probably be hacked. No, the type that are hardwired and secure. It was just a thought." I knew it was a good idea but an expensive one. Dani didn't respond. I was hoping I hadn't offended her.

I continued to think on solutions, not firm on any particular notions.

A week later Dani called me very excited. It was nice to get a call that didn't involve some sort of crisis. "You need to come and see this."

"What Dani? What do you want me to see?"

"I can't tell you. It's a surprise. Can you just drive by?"

"Sure," I replied. "I will be by in a few minutes."

I drove over to Dani's home with a mind full of curiosity. The area was continuing to grow, new houses being built continually and people moving in all around them. Maybe what was exciting her was that she would have a new neighbor, someone that could help them watch the house. I even thought that maybe the police were there and they had caught someone pounding on doors and windows. I found that my anticipation level, as well as my imagination, was increasing the closer I got to her home.

As I drove my car around the corner I was rewarded with seeing a service truck parked in front of the house. Several people were climbing ladders and running wire. Jeff was out with the man that appeared to be in charge, pointing to different places of the house and nodding their heads in agreement. I had no idea what went into it but Dani had taken my idea and somehow convinced Jeff to install security cameras around the house. I was overwhelmed with joy and relief as well as excitement for them. This would certainly help make their home a safer place.

I waved at Jeff as I drove by. He was smiling and waved and then returned with focus on the project at hand. I couldn't see Dani anywhere but I could only assume that she was watching from inside the house through one of the windows. I also thanked the Lord for the idea. I had come to know with assurance that all good things come from Him.

It didn't take long to test out the new security cameras. Several nights after they were installed Dani heard pounding on the door again. This time, however, it was accompanied by angry yelling. Dani told me that she went to the computer screen in the safety of the interior office. There, displaying the video feed from the front camera, was a shadowy figure at the front door pounding and yelling. Obviously, this person felt confident and secure in not being discovered by any neighbors at such a late hour. Then the figure stopped in mid swing. Slowly, and uncomprehendingly at first, the figure turned to look directly at the camera mounted up in the corner of the porch ceiling where Jeff had it positioned to film everything at the front door. Dani told me she had to stifle a scream as she recognized her father's image. Surprise at first reflected on his features then anger and frustration turned his face into a snarling rage. With fist upturned toward the camera as if to say, "I'll get even with you!" the figure turned and disappeared into the night.

Even though she was watching safely behind locked doors Dani told me how her skin crawled and her stomach knotted up with fear. It was not that the camera had captured a digital image of a possible intruder, but she told me that it was that fact that she knew the person. She knew the face and she also knew all too well the meaning of the raised fist. She said she knew the price she would pay if she were alone with him again. For that moment, she was glad Jeff had installed the cameras. She felt that she and her family were safer.

I was about to try to convince her that now that we had him on tape, pounding on the door, yelling at her, that it was the right time to go to the police. Surely, they could see her life might be in danger. Then, I realized that we really didn't have anything but a man pounding on the door. No forced entry, no physical abuse, and no law breaking. Even with this disappointment, I realized that the most important priority had been achieved. Dani and her children were safer than they had been in months. If there was a break-in or a theft then it would be caught on tape, the alarm would go off, and the security company would dispatch the police. Time would prove their undoing if they decided to breech the home once more. They would have to do it another way. We were slowly plugging holes in a dangerous dyke to prevent a major flood. Plugging one more hole had lessened the power and control over Dani a bit more.

Dani also told me about a strange thing that happened about a week later. It was a Saturday afternoon and Jeff was home from work. The doorbell rang and Jeff was greeted by a man at the door with scruffy hair, partial beard, and worn jeans. He introduced himself as a supervisor with the security company. He indicated that several customers in the area were experiencing outages and he was sent out to check out their security equipment to ensure that everything was working alright. Maybe it was the man's appearance or just a gut feeling, but Jeff was cautious. He asked the man to wait for a minute or two on the porch. Jeff stepped back into the house and called the security company on his cell phone to corroborate the man's story. The security company indicated that there were no outages in his area and they did not have a supervisor in his area that day. Worried and concerned, Jeff turn back to the door to confront the man only to hear squealing tires and saw the tail end of a car disappearing around the corner. Dani asked me what I thought it meant. The only thing I could think of was a botched attempt made by her dad to somehow circumvent the security system. Since the system was hardwired instead of wireless, the possibilities of hacking the system was very slight indeed.

The security cameras did their job. There was no more pounding on doors and or people lurking around the house. Occasionally the cameras would pick up someone walking around the house, but they avoided looking at the cameras and were never there very long. It was evident that her dad was not going to give up easily.

I felt like I was facing an opponent in a chess game, each of us making a move and anticipating the next. But this was not a game. It was real. I just hoped that the Lord would help me stay one step ahead of him. What was going to be his next move?

CHAPTER 12

The Rules

"We can complain because rose bushes have thorns or we can rejoice because thorn bushes have roses."
—Abraham Lincoln

Dani pushed the cart through the narrow aisles of the store. Searching for clothes for the kids was never easy. They were growing so fast and each preferred only certain colors. It seemed like they could even outgrow their own size before even getting home, and the cost seemed to increase by the day. It was enough to make one's head swim. The kids with their enthusiasm and youthful rambunctiousness didn't make shopping any easier.

Jenny and Cami ran ahead to the toy section leaving her with Jake in the cart. She didn't worry about them because they knew they needed to stay together, and, besides, she might get her shopping done quicker with fewer distractions.

"Don't you move!" she said sternly to Jake, "I will be right here." Dani approached a circular rack and made her way around to the back side of the rack to see the sizes she was trying to find. This way, she could shop and keep an eye on cute little Jake at the same time.

Without any warning, someone grabbed Dani's arm in a powerful grip. The pain brought tears to her eyes. She was about to turn to see the source of the pain when she heard a whisper in her ear. She instantly recognized the voice.

"Did you forget the rules?" the raspy voice whispered.

Even though Dani couldn't see the person behind her, the voice paralyzed her with fear. She couldn't run, she couldn't scream, and all she could do was shake her head. Again, the voice whispered in her ear.

"Have you been talking about me?"

She shook her head again. She knew it was a lie but she had to protect her children and the bishop.

"You better not be telling him! If you tell him we will arrange a meeting with him in the parking lot after church. It won't be a pretty sight when we get done," he continued to whisper close to the back of her ear. "You might even find someone much closer suffering like you did. Do you want that?"

Dani glanced over at Jake. She knew the voice was speaking of him. Jake was sitting in the cart sucking on a bottle, oblivious to what was going on. Dani shook her head once more. She tried unsuccessfully not to show her fear.

The voice behind her whispered a single word in her ear, then suddenly the painful grip released and she felt his presence move away from her.

"Are you finding everything alright?' A smartly dressed woman with *Judy* on her name tag appeared at the rack. Dani now realized why the man with the painful grip left. He must have seen the salesperson coming. "They are marked way down for clearance."

Dani gave a sigh of relief. She thanked the clerk and moved over to the cart with Jake sitting so content. Her fear suddenly changed to panic. What about Jenny and Cami? Her concerns were now for her other two children. Had he found them? Were they okay?

She pushed the cart almost at a run. Her eyes darted in and out of the isles trying to catch a glimpse of the man. As she approached the toy section she was starting to panic. Why did she leave them alone? She blamed herself for being so foolish and stupid. Why wasn't she more careful? They should have all stayed together. As she arrived in the toy section she started to scan down the isles looking for her children. Where were they? Had they been taken? She thought to herself that she would gladly give her own life for them. Let them be here God, please!

She was at the last aisle now. Panic was then replaced by a flood of relief. There they were, sitting on the floor having a disagreement over a toy. They were safe! Thank you, God!

"Children," she said in the calmest voice she could muster. "Time to go. Please! Now!"

Cami was about ready to throw the toy to the side when she noticed the stern look on her mother's face. Carefully she put the toy back on the rack. She and Jenny got up and followed their mom out of the store. Sensing that their mom was worried neither of them protested about leaving the store.

Dani didn't feel safe until she reached home and locked the door behind her and reengaged the security system. Even then she could still feel the pain in her arm and the echo of the voice in her ear.

Something deep inside her, a feeling or compulsion she could not explain, an overwhelming and controlling feeling that was blocking her ability to choose, told her she had better not tell anyone. As if on cue, she adopted the almost forgotten drooping posture. Her thoughts and her countenance made similar adjustments. Her thoughts recalled the last thing the man had said to her at the store. Mechanically, Dani climbed the stairs to her bedroom. She took a suitcase out of the closet and started packing her clothes neatly within it.

With home prices rising my business had exploded. I was going from appointment to appointment. I spent a lot of time in my mobile office, my car, with my planner, my cell phone and my briefcase. I was putting in some long hours as well as taking care of my ecclesiastical and family duties. Off and on during the day, I had a feeling I should call Dani. As the day went on the feeling became stronger, almost urgent. With my last appointment canceling, I had some unscheduled time so I pulled into a shopping center parking lot, parked in a shady spot, and dialed Dani's number. It went right to voice mail.

I waited for a few minutes and tried again with the same result. I was about to drive on to my next appointment when I remembered that sometimes she would respond to a text when she wouldn't answer the phone.

"RUOK?" I entered the abbreviated message into the phone and pressed send. Then I waited.

After a few more minutes, again there was still no answer. I wondered why the feeling had been so strong. Shrugging my shoulders, I engaged the drive gear to the engine and started pulling out of the parking space when my phone rang a musical tone. The message was from Dani. The message simply said, "No."

I put my car back into park and typed back a response.

"What is wrong?"

"Nothing," came back the reply. Everything inside me told me that something was wrong. Even though text messages are devoid of emotion, I could feel it strong in this one word.

"Whatever it is you can tell me," I sent the message in reply.

"I can't tell you. I can't tell anyone."

"Why not?" I asked.

"I just can't. It is against the rules."

"What rules?" I asked. I was relieved that at least she was talking to me. But there was no reply. Obviously, I asked the wrong question.

"You have always been able to tell me anything," I sent again.

There was a long pause before the next reply, as if she were thinking and considering.

"Is it safe?"

She had stopped asking me that question during our sessions months ago. Something was really wrong.

"Yes, it is safe!"

Again, there was a long pause. I thought for sure she was going to pull away. Whatever had happened must have been serious. Finally, after what seemed like an eternity came a response.

"I have to go back."

"Go back where?" I asked, my fingers typing a response as fast as possible.

"To him," she replied.

"To who? Your father?" Again, a long pause.

"Yes," came the single word reply.

"Why?" I couldn't believe this. Why? Why would she knowingly and even willingly go back to abuse? Something must have happened and I needed to find out what had caused this change in her thinking.

"I just have to."

"Why?" I asked again.

"I saw my dad today."

"Did he tell you to go back to him?"

"No."

"Then what did he say?" I was trying to probe just enough to get her to keep communicating with me.

"I do not remember."

In desperation, I struggled to find something to say to get her to tell me something so that I could help her. Heaven forbid, I knew if she went back to her father she would never get out of abuse.

"Did he speak to you?"

"He said something to me."

"What did he say?" I nearly pleaded.

"He said a word to me."

"What was the word?"

"I don't remember."

I was having a difficult time understanding that. If he said something and it affected her this dramatically, she certainly would know what it was.

"Why don't you remember?"

"I don't know. I keep trying to remember. I really do but I can't remember."

"So, what he said is making you feel like you have to go back?" I asked in return.

"Yes. I don't know why. I can't control it. It is something I have to do. I have to go back."

It felt like a viscous loop. No matter how I tried, she always came back to the decision that she had to go back. This word seemed to have control over her. She seemed to be ignoring the relationship with her husband, her children, and her home. At a drop of a word she was willing to go back? It didn't make sense. Something had happened. I had an impression I needed to take control of the situation.

"You don't have to go back." I responded, testing my new approach.

"I don't?" came the reply.

"No, you don't."

"Why?" Then she added "I have to go back."

"But you don't," I sent back.

"Why?" came the response again.

An idea was formulating in my mind. Was it inspiration? I could only think that God had His hand in what I was doing right now. I pressed forward.

"I think that this word is a trigger of some sort."

"A trigger?" she responded.

"A word that you are conditioned to respond to in a certain way."

"Really?" she asked.

"Really," I sent the message back.

"In this case you are supposed to go back. But you don't have to." I sent another.

"I don't have to go back?" she asked after several long minutes.

"No, you don't have to go back."

"But I packed my suitcase."

I couldn't believe it. She had actually packed a suitcase. She really was ready to go back.

"You can unpack it. You don't have to go anywhere."

"Really?" she came back with the text reply.

"Really."

"I am glad," she responded back. "I didn't really want to go back."

"I know," I sent my message back.

After a few minutes, her message came back. I couldn't think of any two words that were more assuring. "Thank you."

I breathed a sigh of relief. Another approaching disaster had been averted. Then, as I gave it some thought, it was God who had intervened to save her life. I said a quick prayer of thanks and pulled out of the parking lot.

The bright light made Dani squint. She was trying to make sense of the chaos around her. One moment she had been nestled beneath the warm blankets in her bed and the next she was standing there in the middle of the bedroom in her nightgown. Her father was yelling at her. As the clouds of sleep dissipated, she started making sense of the angry barrage of words coming from his mouth.

"You just don't follow the rules!" he yelled at her. "You are so stupid and worthless."

He slapped her on the side of her head. She stumbled briefly and stood back up. From previous experience she knew it would be worse if she lay down or tried to run away.

"Don't you realize there are consequences? What were you thinking?"

He was pacing back and forth. His face was the color of crimson. As his voice level increased her fear went to terror. She had never seen him so angry.

Without warning he punched her in the stomach. She doubled over trying to catch her breath. A kick to her side sent her sprawling into the wall. Stabbing pain shot through her side and up her back. After bouncing against the wall, she cleared her eyes of tears just in time to duck as a book slammed into the wall where her head had been. He was totally out of control and she knew there was no escape.

"You are just a throwaway. Nobody loves you, do you hear? Nobody!"

Dani was waiting for the next aggression to happen and her body tensed in anticipation.

"Why don't you just go away? God doesn't love you. You are just trash. God hates trash!"

In his rage, he grabbed Dani by the arm and flung her. She flew like a rag doll across the room, bounced off the bed, and collided with the corner of the dresser with a sickening thud and an audible crack. Dani lay in a heap at the base of the dresser.

Having satisfied his rage, Dani's father left the room. Without even a glance back he slammed the door behind him.

Slowly Dani became aware that she was alone in the room. She felt pain in several parts of her body which wasn't unusual after a beating. As she moved to sit up, she gave an involuntary scream. Leaning against the dresser, she tenderly touched the source of the pain. Protruding out of the broken skin of her upper arm was something white, a bone would have been her guess although she had never seen one. She felt a bit dizzy not knowing she was going into shock.

From outside the door she could hear yelling. Her mom and dad were in the hallway arguing. Occasionally she could understand words like "trash" or "mistake" and she knew they were talking about her. She wondered why she was even alive. Her parents didn't love her. She was called a "throwaway" and "garbage." Was she really those things? She didn't understand. They said even God thought she was trash. She had tried to be obedient and to do what they asked, but it never seemed to be enough.

The opening of the door broke into her thoughts. They both stood there, not comprehending at first and then anger spread across her mother's face.

"This is your mess! You clean it up," she spit at her husband.

Dani had expected her mother to pick her up, hold her, give her comfort, love her. She did none of these things, instead she turned on her heel and left the room.

On the way to the hospital Dani was grilled about what she should say and do. The pain in her arm was intense. She had remembered her father pacing the room while she sat there cradling her broken arm. She heard him reason with himself out loud. Because she had been told over and over that she was worthless and not wanted, she was not surprised when she heard him try to find a way to leave her the way she was and not get medical attention. He talked about neighbors finding out, or people at church talking, or that the other children would find out and then they would ask why he hadn't taken her to the doctor. No, he had to take her, but how to keep them finding out what had really happened, what he had done. All she could do was wait.

Finally, he had turned to her and said, "Here are the rules! You have to obey the rules, do you understand?"

She nodded. She was beyond pain now, all she wanted to do was sleep. When her eyelids drooped, he yelled at her or kicked her so she would wake up and pay attention.

The car stopped at a light. "Listen, you hear?" Her father's voice had a hint of panic in it. The intensity of his voice caused Dani to open her eyes. "If you don't learn these rules, I will break your other arm, understand?" He got down in her face as he said it. She could feel his hot breath and see the sweat on his red face.

"When we get to the hospital you sit next to me. If they try to take you off alone, you tell them you need me with you. Repeat that!"

Dani did her best to repeat it. The pain and the shock made her thinking fuzzy. She didn't want to see him mad again. She wanted to listen and make her dad happy. The urgency in his voice let her know she wanted to do it right.

"Never look at the doctor or respond to him unless you are told to. Repeat that, now!"

She faltered about half way through the rule and he reached over and squeezed her broken arm. A murmur of pain escaped her lips. She repeated back as best she could. It must have passed his scrutiny because he continued.

He thought for a moment and then said, "If anyone asks you questions, you don't answer, you let me do the talking."

She didn't need to be prompted, she repeated what he said.

After thinking once more he gave her another rule. "Remember, this is all your fault. You were stupid and clumsy and fell off the bed. Repeat it."

Obediently, Dani repeated what she heard. During the rest of the ride she repeated the rules several more times until her father was satisfied there would be no mistakes. As if to make sure the secret would be safe he added one last thing.

"If you tell any of them what happened they will take you away from your mom and me and lock you up in a dark room all by yourself and never let you out. Do you want that?"

She shook her head. She noticed that he was pulling into the hospital parking lot.

"You had better not make a mistake. Understand?"

She was almost too tired and dizzy to answer. She did her best to nod her answer before unconsciousness overcame her.

When Dani came in for her next appointment, I could tell she had been through some sort of an ordeal. She hadn't taken time to comb her blonde hair and her green eyes had dark circles under them telegraphing that she had not been able to sleep much lately. On top of that she looked pale and gaunt. Once more her thin arms were noticeable by the way her shirt hung so loosely on her frame. My heart went out to her. She had the appearance of having undergone a horrible experience one would expect from a prison camp.

Dani wrapped her arms around her legs once more as she sat in the chair at the front of my desk. She didn't speak for several minutes after arriving. I just let her sit there quietly letting her become comfortable with the room and the peace and the quiet hoping it would have some soothing effect on her. I wanted to ask a hundred questions to learn what had happened; to learn what more she had been through.

The memories she was now sharing with me were increasingly more difficult and painful as she dealt with feelings including lack of self-worth, betrayal, and abandonment. When a new memory would come, it undid all the work that had been done to help her understand and cope with the trauma she was forced to relive. Interestingly we could have discussed an incident one evening and overnight a new memory would cause her to forget what I had taught her or she would have completely forgotten what we had discussed. At first, I thought she was either very forgetful or just testing me. Over time my patience level increased as I understood this step in her healing process. The old adage of two steps forward and one step backward mirrored the process that we were experiencing. All in all, I could see that we were making progress.

Each memory seemed to have some sort of strong emotion tied to it. Explaining or defining it eluded me. It was more than just the beatings or the yelling she was describing. There was definitely something more, like some sort of conditioned response, preventing her from telling or sharing it. Usually, when I asked Dani to share something, she would emphatically tell me she could not share it. It would take a lot of coaxing and patience before she would tell me. Had she been threatened? Of that I had little doubt. But still it seemed to be so much stronger or deeper. Some method or technique had been used to shut down her ability to decide on her own. It was almost like her free will had been taken from her.

As I talked with her I found that she had not been eating. I tried to discuss with her how important eating was, a concept that most all of us have no problem with. She told me that she did not feel hungry and didn't want to eat. She told me that she was fat and was eating too much. When she looked in the mirror she saw all of her imperfections and was fat and needed to lose weight or *he* would not be happy. I inquired who he was and she wouldn't say. I knew by this time that it was either caused by recent memories or the recent encounter with her father.

I strongly counseled her to see a doctor. This was way out of my league and I knew she needed medical help. She agreed to see a doctor and we decided to meet in a week and see if her condition had improved. Her health was on the line and if this current course of behavior continued I could only see death being the result. I made sure she promised me she would see a doctor immediately and then I made sure she got home safe.

Our next interview was almost a month later. After we had talked she had been immediately admitted into the hospital. IVs were immediately administered as well as a feeding tube. It appeared that she had been trying to starve herself to death. Somehow in her mind, she was convinced she was fat. No matter how hard she tried she could not lose enough weight. I knew that these thoughts were a result of the memories. It was her father she was trying to lose the weight for and whom she could never please. Her mind was in a constant struggle to distinguish between the past and current reality. I also knew that the longer she was without proper nourishment, the more her mind would be playing tricks on her and she would be susceptible to imagining all sorts of falsehoods.

The month in the hospital allowed the doctors to build her weight back up and get her body responding in a healthy way. This danger seemed to be over for the moment but I knew full well that other dangers lurked right around the corner. I had that feeling you get when you know something bad is going to happen but you just can't put your finger on what it is. For right now Dani was recovering her health enough that the doctors sent her home and removed the feeding tube.

Shortly after she was released, we met in my office. She told me why she had quit eating. It was because of the word or words that her father had whispered into her ear when she saw him while shopping. She still couldn't remember the word but it definitely had left her with a profound feeling of hopelessness. Subconsciously she didn't care about anything except needing to please her father, which meant she had to get the weight off to make him happy. At that point, she lost all caring for those around her and focused only on what her father had said. Nothing else seemed to matter except the implied instructions from the whispered message.

"It was like I didn't have any control over what I wanted to do. I had to do it. I was compelled to go back." She sat there apologizing over and over for worrying me and thanking me for my help. I was just glad she was alive and able to take care of her children again.

The powerful effect this whispered message had on her was pure evil. I remembered hearing about words called *triggers* that were psychologically implanted in a person's mind so that they were compelled to act out a desired set of instructions. This had always been some fictional plot in old spy movies, more Hollywood than reality. What I had recently witnessed was sophisticated and calculated. We needed to find a way to defuse the ticking trigger.

With the security system in and Dani feeling safe now within her own home, I felt it was time to bring in the police to report her dad as being an abuser. At the very least, we could report it and obtain a restraining order to help protect her. I would definitely feel a lot better about Dani's safety if her father was in jail.

At the very mention of it, however, she went into a panic. I quickly regretted my decision to discuss this issue with her. In my wildest dreams, I had no idea I would receive this type of response.

"No, No!" Dani was emphatic. "We can't do it. I can't do it!" There was great emphasis on the *I*. "You just don't understand."

I let the air settle for a minute or two before I spoke.

"Dani?" I asked softly, "What don't I understand?"

When she spoke, it was barely audible as her head was pressed into her legs with her sad eyes peering over her knees.

"It won't work. I have tried it before." She had tears forming in the corners of her eyes.

"Help me understand," I responded cautiously. "What have you tried before?"

"I tried it before," she repeated. "It won't work. It will end badly."

"Please tell me. What have you tried before?" I asked again patiently, keeping my voice low and calm.

"I didn't want to tell you. I was afraid you wouldn't want to help me anymore."

I just sat there waiting for more. She really was afraid. I didn't want to rush her and maybe cause her to shut down altogether. There was definitely something she hadn't told me.

She hung her head in her hands. After a few minutes, she raised her head showing fear filled eyes and began slowly to explain what was scaring her so much.

"I remember being seven or eight. My dad was taking me somewhere. He got really mad at me when I asked where we were going. He said he had had enough of me and that I had no right to ask. I wasn't listening. I didn't learn from my mistakes. I was worthless and didn't even deserve to live. The longer the ride, the madder he became. 'I am going to fix you for good,' he said. 'I am putting you in the psych ward. I've told them to give you shock treatments. They are going to give you the whole works. When you come back, you will be compliant.' He had a strange look on his face. It was different, like he was mad but enjoying it.

"When we pulled up to the front door, he wouldn't even go in with me. He told me they were expecting me. He pointed to the door and told me to go through and down the hall to the nurse's station.

"Don't you think that this is a bit much for a seven-year-old girl to do?" she paused in her story to ask.

I nodded while trying to picture her walking alone and scared down the hallway, no comfort or support from a parent. I couldn't imagine a parent doing such a horrible thing. I would have been terrified finding myself in that situation.

"As I got out of the car he told me to remember the rules."

Here she was mentioning the rules again. What were these rules? Why did they have so much power over her?

"I didn't want to get out of the car. He pushed me out and laughed when he told me that the shock treatments would make me more compliant. I didn't even know what that meant. He laughed again and said, 'Get out you little bitch!'

"I walked up to the door and looked back. He was still there. He yelled at me through the open window to go in. I was scared but I went in. At the end of the long hallway was a desk and behind it a woman in a white uniform. She asked me a lot of questions and took me to a small room. A man came in and asked me more questions. He must have been a doctor because he was telling the nurse what to do. He shook his head as he was reading the papers in a file in front of him. He kept looking at me and then read again. He then told the nurse that they weren't going to do the shock treatments because he could find no reason for them. He said that something must have been wrong with the orders, they had to be incorrect.

"Then he knelt down in front of me and said kind words to me. He said he was sorry, that I shouldn't be there but they had to keep me for observation for a couple of days. I don't remember much more except that all the time I was there, my mom or dad never came to visit me.

"Is that normal?" she asked pausing again in her story.

Normal? It was obvious that Dani's life had been anything but normal. She had experienced a life of chaos and now she was trying to define what normal was. I was sure she observed other families wondering if these things happened in their families as well. I was pleased that she was starting to see the difference.

"No, Dani, that is not normal. I took one of my kids to the doctor with asthma once. She was almost sixteen and could hardly breathe. I carried her from the car into the clinic. I stayed right with her until I could take her home. So, no, I know that what you experienced was not normal. What would you do if that was one of your children?"

Dani thought for a minute, weighing past experience with what she would do. "I would do what you did." Her eyes were sad and hurt. I knew what the next question was going to be.

"Well, I didn't go home in a few days. I think my father objected to the doctor's diagnosis. I was there a month or two. It was a long time away from my family. They didn't give me shock treatments but they did put me on medications that made me tired and sluggish."

"Why was he so mean?" she asked.

I sincerely wished I had an answer for her. How could anyone be so insensitive and cruel to a young, innocent girl? Comprehending it was nearly impossible, so having reasons for such violent abuse just weren't available. This entire experience was foreign to the world I knew.

I questioned why her father had sent her to a psychiatric hospital if there was nothing wrong with her. Did he think something was wrong? That didn't make sense because he would have gone in with her. Was his motive more sinister? Probably. And why would he or her regular doctor insist on electric shock treatments? Here was cruelty heaped onto abuse.

"But I don't see how this relates to what you said about it being tried before." I was trying to find the logic in this story and understand why she was telling me about it.

"I am getting to that. Shortly after Jeff and I were married," she continued, "I was having terrible nightmares. I went to my bishop for help. He was a very nice man like you. When I told him about my dad, he reported it. There was an investigation. The police were called in as well as my mom and dad. When they were confronted with what my bishop had reported, they denied it all. They both lied and supported each other's story."

I started to see where this was headed. "So, your dad told them you were a bit crazy and mentioned that you spent time in a psych ward. That was easily checked by the police. He was able to discredit your accusations and make you appear to be the crazy one, right?"

Dani nodded.

"And I am also going to guess that your bishop quit helping you."

She nodded again. Sadness and hopeless resignation filled her searching eyes.

"Afterwards," she continued, "my dad beat me. He really beat me." She paused and looked at the door again like she used to. "He told me that if I ever did that again he would kill me and throw me out in the garbage."

I sat there processing this new information. What should I do? Did this change anything and if it did, how? I was seeing another side of her father, a very dangerous side. He was calculating and diabolical. He appeared to cover and protect himself at every turn. All I was trying to do was help this tormented young mother through a tough time and now it had gotten very complicated. Taking this to the police appeared to not be an option. With just her word alone I wouldn't be taken seriously. Unless I had a lot more concrete evidence, he would walk away again.

Dani could see that I was mulling over what she had just shared. Then she spoke with hopeless expectation.

"Are you going to stop helping me?"

CHAPTER 13

New Rules

> *"The only thing necessary for the triumph of evil is that good men do nothing"*
> —EDMUND BURKE

Dani was sitting in a room with other children of various ages. There had been no light, no windows or doors. After a while most of the children were crying and screaming with fear. This went on for what seemed to be forever until the door opened and everyone squinted because of the light flooding through the door. A man stepped in and told the children if they wanted to get out of the dark room and get something to eat that they had to do everything they were told, no matter what. These children started crawling or walking to the door as if to say they had learned the lesson. Dani didn't cry or scream. She simply wasn't afraid of the dark. She had already spent countless hours in a closet with little or no light. She did, however, fear the man far more than the dark. Even though she was not crying, she was allowed to leave like the rest. She was just glad to be out of the room.

Then she was led with some older children to a room with a television. The images on the screen were strange to Dani. Even though she rarely got the chance to watch television, she knew there was definitely something strange with this program. There was no color and the images looked really old. Vertical lines were showing on the sides of the screen like it was worn out.

She didn't want to watch this television program but she was being forced to. If her attention strayed she would get a kick or hit to ensure she was watching everything. Sometimes she would get a kick even when she was making sure she was watching. She didn't really understand what she was seeing, however, if she paid attention her father seemed happier, or at least she was less apt to receive the evidence of his displeasure.

On the screen Dani saw men in light colored uniforms. They appeared to be short and walked very stiffly. They wore funny little hats that reminded her of her brother's baseball cap. She also noticed that when she saw their faces they had slanted eyes and when they spoke she could not understand what they were saying.

Two of these strange men were pulling and dragging another man between them. He was taller than the rest and looked tired and ragged. He had an unkempt beard unlike his captors who had smooth facial skin. They dragged him to a door, opened it, and threw him inside a room. The camera followed him in revealing that the room was completely dark. There were no windows or other doors visible. One man said a sharp unintelligible word and the camera was removed, the door was closed and locked with the bearded man inside. After a space of time she could hear the man screaming. Two of the uniformed men came to the door, spoke to each other, then nodded and smiled broadly.

The scene on the television had changed to a different room. The same bearded man was dragged in and strapped down to a table. She could see the fear in his eyes seeing only the whites of his eyes as they darted back and forth in horrible anticipation of some pending doom. Then the uniformed men brought some cables over and attached the two cables to each of his hands. The end of the cables went to a black box with silver nubs on the top.

She heard a man behind her ask, "That's a regular car battery, right?"

The other man simply grunted in agreement.

Dani watched a man attach the cable to the battery and instantly the man screamed and his body jerked and trembled violently. It was a horrible and frightening sound. She had never before heard anything like it. Without learning if the man was okay she was grabbed by an arm and pulled down a hallway.

"Now it's your turn, you worthless throwaway." His voice had an edge to it that Dani didn't like.

As they entered the room he kicked her and told her to lay down on the floor. She obeyed. Her fear rose as he brought the heavy cables over. Remembering what happened to the television man her fear escalated.

"Here, hold this," he demanded. "And don't let go, hear?" She complied to the commands, grabbing the extended cable in her right hand.

Then he knelt beside her and said a word to her. He had her repeat it over and over.

"When you hear this word, I want you to remember how worthless you are. Nobody loves you! Remember you belong to me. I own you! You don't have a right to ever leave me. And you have to do what I say!"

A second cable was forced into her other hand. Then without warning, the man connected the cables to the battery sending jolts of electric current through her. She felt pain throughout every inch of her body. Dani wanted to scream but she couldn't. Breathing was impossible. Her little body jerked uncontrollably and her teeth chattered. After what seemed like an eternity it all stopped. She lay there trying to catch her breath and get her bearings once more. She felt pain through all of her body.

Then he repeated the process. He said a word, attaching to it demeaning and cruel labels, then added his ownership. Once more he attached the cable again. Dani lost track of how many times or how long it lasted and finally fell into unconsciousness. Her last thought just before the darkness welcomed her was that she wished she were dead.

Was I going to continue to help Dani? There was no other answer possible: Of course, I was going to continue helping her. She literally had no one in her life who believed in her. Jeff was a good husband but he didn't want to hear about her past or about the abuse and simply couldn't handle it. Much like the adage of the ostrich hiding its head in the sand, if he didn't see it, it didn't exist! She had brothers and sisters but they didn't keep in touch, except to send her notes and leave messages on her phone about how un-Christlike and anti-family she was and how much she was hurting her mom and dad by not seeing them. If her father was indeed an abuser and her mom supported her husband either by ignorance or by choice, it still meant that Dani had no one to protect her or to keep her safe. If I wasn't there, I wondered how long it would be before she was back into that abusive situation. I appeared to be her only link between old memories and reality – between abuse and safety.

In addition, during my recent interview, Dani revealed that even though the security cameras had prevented her dad and others from approaching the house, it did not prevent them from parking just out of sight of the outside cameras. There were two cars that were always there and they parked as if the occupants were just watching the house. Occasionally there would be a police car from another city parked just down the street. For what reason? It was obvious they were watching and yet they did not approach the house. Was their motive to watch her movements and map when she was coming and going? Or was it for intimidation and sending her a message? The recent incident where he had whispered a word into her ear nearly causing her to drop everything, pack her bags, abandon her family, and go back to him, really had me concerned. This was sophisticated control and very effective. Where had he learned techniques like that and how deep did they go to controlling her? I had no clue how to undo some sort of trigger like that. I also knew that if I didn't know then I knew someone who did, God!

Dani had shared a recent memory with me shortly after our last conversation. In this memory, she was being forced to watch a TV program with uniformed soldiers and a bearded man who was tortured. As she described the types of torture she had watched I could only surmise that her father had somehow obtained an old Japanese war torture training film. From her description, the soldiers sure seemed to be World War II era and the bearded man most likely a captured soldier on whom they were experimenting with different kinds of torture and mind control techniques. Dani had obviously been the recipient of some of these techniques. Who knows what else she had been through? It was very effective and horrific that this was done on such a young girl. The results had been enough to almost cause a married mother of three to leave everything good she knew with the whisper of a word. All of this happened because a trigger word had been set during some sort of torture. Unbelievable!

The very idea that her father had done these things to a little girl – for any reason – really incensed me. How could her father, any father, do such things? It really was a miracle that Dani wasn't in some sort of institution. The more I learned about her past, the more amazing and almost unbelievable it became. Even more disturbing was her memory that other children were being subjected to this type of conditioning. Who were they? More importantly, where were they?

In the beginning, her memories were just shadowy fragments. Now they were memories revealing very horrific events resulting from the fury of the abuser. Their frequency seemed to be never ending. We would deal with one memory only to have another take its place. The abuse Dani had gone through must have lasted decades. The sheer number of abusive events that she had suppressed totaled far more than either of us could imagine.

It was almost as though Dani had suppressed the worst memories the deepest because each new memory became increasingly worse. I marveled at how God had provided a way for Dani to survive all this without going insane. In His wisdom, it appeared that she was able to bury these memories that were just too horrible to understand at her age. The unfortunate side effect was that in order for Dani to go through the healing process it became apparent that she had to re-experience them. My hope was that eventually we would reach the bottom of the memory barrel. I really hoped this would be soon for both our sakes.

What Dani needed was some help to break through *the rules*. They seemed to govern her life and her actions. I had no idea how to counteract the triggers but I knew God did. I was inspired that what Dani needed to do was replace these rules with a new set of rules. This would provide a new way for Dani to make correct decisions when faced with an old rule.

The wait for assistance in the clinic seemed intolerably long. Other people were there as well. One man was moaning and holding his leg. A woman was holding a baby that was crying and screaming. Nurses were running around making sure paperwork was being completed and patients calmed until they could be seen. The phone was ringing continually even though a nurse was talking nonstop on call after call.

Dani watched all of this while she held a towel on her arm. The towel was becoming soaked with blood. She sat next to her father who was a mixture of fear and apprehension. He watched the organized chaos and it was difficult for Dani to determine if her dad was concerned about her or something else. Her arm throbbed and she tried not to show she was in pain. Even though she tried to stop them, she could not prevent the tears from welling up in her eyes.

"Remember the rules!" he told her in a low voice. "Don't look at the doctor or nurse because they will see right through you. They will know what kind of dirty person you are. They won't believe you anyway."

At that moment, a police officer walked through the front door. He seemed to have no particular purpose as he walked through observing the rush of professionals taking care of patients. Her dad nudged her and at the same time pointed to the police officer.

"Remember it is all your fault," Her father reinforced the lie once more.

"Don't look at the cop either. If he looks you in the eye he will see what a worthless and dirty piece of garbage you are and he will take you away from me and put you in a dark room all by yourself. Do you want that?"

Holding her painful arm tighter, Dani shook her head and averted her eyes from the policeman. She had learned from her father that policemen were people to be feared. He had told her that if she tried to tell her dad's secrets to the police officer, that he wouldn't believe her and would use his gun to shoot her. Dani would be just as glad if he didn't come anywhere near them.

"Remember the rule when the doctor comes. You did this to yourself. You are clumsy and stupid. Understand?"

Dani nodded. She remembered earlier that evening her dad holding her arm in a vice-like grip with one hand and cutting her arm with a knife in the other. The knife went deep and the pain was unreal. She wanted to scream but she knew better. Her free hand clinched the chair she was sitting on to help redirect the pain. He seemed to have some sort of smile on his face. Crimson fluid oozed from the wound. She wanted to resist, to run away, but she couldn't. As the pain increased the expression on his face changed from one of pleasure to that of fear. He saw what he had done and how deep the cut was and he realized he had gone too far.

A uniformed nurse approached her father and held her hand out and asked, "Have you completed the forms?"

Without speaking her dad's expression changed. He adopted a stern look and handed her the clipboard. The nurse reviewed the forms on all sides.

"She did this to herself?" the nurse asked with a strong note of skepticism.

Her father must have picked up on it because he went into a long description of how much difficulty he and her mother have had with her. She was always hurting herself and it was such a burden on the family. He even mentioned she had been in a psych ward and how the professionals there couldn't even help her.

The nurse interrupted, "It says here that she is allergic to any medication that numbs the skin?"

"Yes," he answered with an edge to his voice. "Very."

Dani didn't dare look her in the eye. Believing what her father had told her, she was afraid that the nurse would see right through her. In her mind, she remembered very clearly her father telling her not to ask for medications because she didn't deserve them. She didn't understand why. Maybe it was because she was dirty and worthless.

Moments later Dani was seated in a room beneath bright lights. A young doctor was cleaning out the wound and shook his head because it was so deep. He started cauterizing and layering stitches to close the wound so it could begin the healing process. As he was stitching she started to cry because the pain was so intense due to the lack of any pain killers. At one point, Dani stole a glance at the doctor's face and she could even see tears in his eyes as well.

She glanced at her father, standing against the wall expressionless and emotionless watching every move and listening to every word. Again, the feeling of hopelessness welled up inside her. Hopelessness and pain seemed to be her lot at the moment. She cried again.

As Dani received memories we discussed them. She was extremely fearful to share some of them with me. I now knew it was because of the triggers. I also realized that the triggers were placed to protect the abuser from being exposed. This knowledge enabled me to be patient and to not push too far for answers or responses.

The other amazing thing that I attribute totally to the love and mercy of the Lord Jesus Christ, was that once she shared a memory and in a sense suffered again the incident, the memory was lifted from her and she didn't seem to remember it again. If she did remember it, her response was much different and without all the emotion and pain attached to it. Through the atonement of Jesus Christ, the pain that had been buried for years was being taken away by a loving Savior. As our journey progressed, I noticed changes happening within Dani. She appeared to have more self-confidence and happiness. The pain she had been experiencing had been replaced with love and peace.

Amid all this turmoil she found it important to tell me that she did not harbor ill feelings toward her father and mother; she just didn't want to be abused anymore. In Matthew Jesus said,

> *Take my yoke upon you, and learn of me;*
> *for I am meek and lowly in heart: and ye shall find rest*
> *unto your souls. For my yoke is easy,*
> *and my burden is light.*
> –Matthew 11:29 KJV

I was witnessing the blessing of visibly seeing her burdens being lifted right before my very eyes.

A few weeks later I decided to ask her about the rules that seemed to keep coming up in her memories. She would indicate that sometimes she still followed these rules out of habit. It was my opinion that they were followed out of a conditioned response. Even though she was hesitant to share the rules, she started telling me about them.

"These rules have been so present in almost every memory we have talked about," she began. "When the memories came last night, and now even throughout the day, I realized how many of them I still follow. He started telling them to me when I was very small. The list grew as I did. But there is a lot of fear tied to it."

"Did you bring a list of these with you?" I asked. She didn't bring the usual notebook.

"I don't need a list. I can recall every one of them. They were all reinforced very regularly." She sat there expressionless but with a hint of sadness in her eyes. "Is it still safe for me to share?"

I nodded in the affirmative.

"I will just start telling you about them. That would be the easiest. Okay?"

I nodded again as she started listing these rules from memory.

"Don't question anything."

"Don't get personal with anyone. No one cares about you, so why bother? Never believe what anyone says. They'll lie to you. They'll make you think you are worth something and you're not."

She paused, not so much because she was trying to remember, which I was convinced she wasn't, but to make sure I didn't have any questions. Then she continued.

"There can only be one thing on my plate. I don't deserve any more. This was like a roll, or some corn, or a piece of chicken, never all of it or more than one thing. That was difficult watching my family eat all they wanted. Even today there are times that I only put one item on my plate."

"Don't look people in the eye. They'll see right through you."

"Don't talk unless you have permission."

"Don't eat in public. Everyone will see what a pig you are."

"His truth is the only truth. That was my father's truth, by the way."

She paused again. "The next one is difficult because you have taught me so much and this goes against what you taught me. At first, I didn't know if you were telling me the truth. I didn't want to believe you because of the rules. I want to thank you for teaching me truth." Her thanks were spontaneous and sincere.

"No praying unless he, my father, was with me. I remember when I was older he started this one, when I was ten or eleven. He would say that God wouldn't hear me anyway. I remember kneeling next to him. He would say the words to me and then I would say them to God. He would always make me ask him for forgiveness: for making him angry, or not being obedient, or not listening, for asking too much, or for not taking care of myself, or not being respectful, for being demanding, for whining, for complaining, for being dirty, and for making too many mistakes."

I was having a difficult time believing what I was hearing. Not that I thought she wasn't being truthful but that this had happened right here in my community. I had heard about similar things happening in faraway places. To be happening right here and right now was very sobering to me.

"No asking God for help. He won't listen, he won't help someone like me.

"No Scriptures or church stuff unless he gives it to me.

"No reading church stuff unless he is with me.

"No sacrament. I am too dirty, too worthless, and too evil for things like that. I think that is why for the longest time after I was married I would take the piece of bread and put it in my pocket or I put it in my mouth so my kids would think I took it. Then I would take it out later without them noticing and put it into a tissue.

"I only get one blanket. If I am cold it is my own fault.

"I only get the crust of the bread. That was the part that my siblings didn't like. When my mom would make lunch she usually had a pile of crusts left over and she would tell my dad to give it to me. Sometimes he did willingly, most of the time he said I had to earn it. I still do that. Jeff or the kids will get the loaf out and all the crust will be gone.

"I have to always wash my hands before I could touch him. He made me because he said I was dirty trash. He didn't want my filth all over him.

"No kissing anyone on the lips EVER. I remember getting hit over and over when he would tell me that. He said that kissing was only something he could do. He said it was a special thing just between he and I."

That rule struck me hard. Did her dad have a fixation for her? Was that the secret he had been trying to hide all these years? Was he really a pedophile?

"Anything in the trash is fair game. He would beat me for getting into the pantry or the fridge. He said I could have whatever I wanted as long as I found it in the trash. That is something I still do. I still get some food from the trash when no one is looking." She dropped her eyes as if in embarrassment.

"I could have only one pair of shoes, and I had to ask for them. He started this one when I wore them to bed and tried to kick him. After that he would take them from me and if I wanted them I had to ask for them. Sometimes he wouldn't give them back, and I had to go without.

"I had to ask permission to use the bathroom. If he wasn't available to come, or to let me out of my room or the closet, then I didn't get to go. I remember when I did get to go, he would yell at me if I was taking too long. He would stand there and smack me in the head or chest until I got off.

"I could only shower with his permission. I remember most of the time he would give me just a few minutes. If I wasn't fast enough he would yell at me and then turn the water off. It didn't really matter if I got all the soap off or not. I had to be done.

"I could only have my contact lenses when I had to go somewhere. I remember him breaking my glasses in half. He said that I looked like a freak in them. My mom made him get me contacts so I could see at school. He would tell me that he didn't have time to mess with my sh** and so I could only wear them when I absolutely had to.

"No whining.

"No complaining.

"No crying.

"No talking to boys. Not at school or at church or anywhere. As I got older, I remember him beating me and making me promise that I wouldn't talk to boys. He said if I did he would find out. He said he would always be watching. He said that if they knew what I really was they would run. He told me that boys thought I was fat, ugly, and stupid so don't even bother.

"Because he was my father and the priesthood holder, he said he could do what he wanted.

"He always comes first. No questions.

"Everything has to be earned. No questions"

When Dani finished, we both sat there in silence digesting this huge list of don'ts. She was studying my expression to see if I was shocked or surprised. I was both quite frankly, however, it was essential for her that I kept my personal feelings hidden. I knew she needed to know that she wasn't strange or weird or that I was shocked.

I was shocked! Really shocked! Blood boiling shocked. Dani's father had risen to a new level of power and control. He not only wanted to have power and control over her life but he wanted to control every aspect of her life. He dictated when she could eat and how much, when to use the bathroom, even what she could think and believe. The list really did grow as she got older. He forced more extreme measures including not ever speaking to other children or adults. He demanded complete control over her as she got older and could have started thinking for herself. Absolute terror isolated her from those who could help her such as the police and school teachers.

Great lengths were taken to prevent her from having any opportunity to tell anyone about her life. When I had heard about kidnapping or abuse stories, I wondered why the victims did not just yell out or run from the abuser. Now I was beginning to understand how these rules and Dani's indoctrination by her father created complete control of her activities, thoughts, and ideas. Even what she could eat and how much made her so completely dependent on him that she could not, even would not, consider leaving him or seeking help. I could now see why victims of this type of abuse don't escape of their own volition.

Her father had done such a complete and total job of controlling Dani's life that even now in her adulthood and without him being physically in her daily life, he still had an amazing amount of control over her thinking and behavior. Her actions and thinking had to work their way through some sort of a manipulating control panel first. There seemed to be a hierarchy of control triggers set by prior torture and brainwashing.

I tried to focus my anger away from her father and what should happen to him for all the horrible and evil things he had done to her. Every fiber of my soul told me to focus my energies on helping Dani to overcome these rules and triggers and provide her with enough knowledge, understanding, courage, and faith to be able to stay out of abuse, diffuse the triggers, and not go back under any circumstances. I had to find my own solace through the Infinite Atonement.

"I think I know what we need to do," I said, recalling my earlier impression.

"What is that?" she asked inquisitively.

Heaven-sent ideas were starting to formulate in my head. Could it really be that simple? I was outlining in my mind a way to combat evil at its core and allow Dani the framework to stay free from the abuse.

"I think," I responded after a moment's thought, "you need a new set of rules."

The smile on her face told me that she agreed. She understood rules. She was used to following them. She would just need to have a reason to replace the old rules. Following a new set of rules designed to protect her and her family and keep her safe looked like just the reason. To follow the new set of rules, she would just need to believe in God and desire to protect her family. I believed in God and knew that He did not want her to go back into abuse. I found myself praying for God to assign a few angels to watch after Dani and her family.

"First of all, I am concerned with your safety. You have had several close calls and if this is any indication of the type of men who are watching you, I would venture a guess that they won't quit their stakeouts. So first some safety rules."

Dani leaned forward with anticipation. There was an obvious look of excitement on her face. Someone was listening to her, believed in her, and was looking out for her benefit and safety. She was totally focused on what I would tell her next.

"Never go anywhere alone. You have to take one or two children with you at all times."

"Why?" she asked.

"These men, your father, are cowards at heart. That is why they sneak up on you and why he locked you up in your room or a closet and hid you from the world. He is afraid to draw attention to himself. So, in addition to taking children with you, always go to public places where there are a lot of people."

She smiled and nodded with understanding.

"Next, I would like you to teach your children to do one thing."

Her eyebrows raised and a slight smile started on the corners of her mouth.

"I want you to teach them to scream. And scream very loud!"

"Why?" she asked again smiling. I knew that it would sound funny.

"When someone approaches you that you don't know and they want you to go with them or split you up or harm you, all of you need to scream. Scream at the top of your lungs. I promise you, nobody will want to come near you. You will be safe."

Dani laughed out loud. I am sure she was envisioning the kids screaming and the reactions of people around her. It did sound outlandish but I knew it would work.

"Can you do that?" I asked.

"Yes," she said. "I think the kids will have a great time practicing that!"

We both laughed. For the first time in weeks I felt a level of confidence that we were moving in the right direction for bringing and keeping Dani out of abuse. We discussed additional rules to help her, such as being aware of those around her when she got out of the car, and being careful when she pulled up to her home making certain that nobody was possibly hiding and waiting in the shadows. I was grateful that she now had some tools that would give her the power to have some control over her own life.

CHAPTER 14

God, Where Are You?

"In the darkest hour the soul is replenished and given strength to continue and endure."
–Dalai Lama

The sound of voices awakened Dani from dozing. With her life in a closet she lost track of time. Sometimes days would pass by before she would see anyone. She knew it must be early evening because the light filtered through the bedroom window and then through the cracks of the closet door. For a brief time each day, she had enough light in her small living space so that she could do her homework without opening the door and feeling the consequences of such an action. On school days, she would go in the door and right to her bedroom when returning home. She would carefully remove all of her clothes except her underwear, and lay them on the bed. Then she would enter the closet and close the door. She didn't say a word to her mother or her siblings because that wasn't allowed. She did this each day, always in the same order without variation. She knew what would happen if she missed one step. This changed on the weekends, which meant she didn't ever leave the closet unless her father had her put on the same dress she wore every day and go with him to church.

As she sat in the closet she could hear her mother's voice as well as those of other women coming in through the front door. She heard words like *Relief Society* and *Presidency* and *meeting* and she knew they were there for one of the meetings that her mother had weekly. Her mother seemed to be in charge because she did most of the talking.

Dani should feel guilty for listening to their conversation but she had no choice. Their voices were clear even though she was in the back of the house. She knew they would be there for a while, then her siblings would come home from playing with friends, and then her father would arrive and they would have dinner. She longed for the days when she would eat dinner with the rest of the family or even eat dinner at all. This family routine was regular and she could almost set her watch by it - that is, if she had a watch.

Her mother said something and the ladies all laughed. The she spoke about love and compassion and how they could help other women. Dani didn't really understand what they were talking about, she just knew it didn't apply to her. She also heard children's voices. Then everything got quiet, and she heard the words of a prayer and a final *amen*. Even though she had been beaten for praying she still said silent prayers in her head. She didn't know why. It just felt right.

After dinner was complete and her sibling's voices seemed to retreat to the back yard, she heard footsteps approach and the door opened.

"Get out here!" her mother barked.

Dani scrambled to her feet and exited the closet.

"Go get something to eat and be quick about it."

In only her underwear her bare feet barely made a sound on the floor as she walked into the kitchen and over to the garbage can. She lifted the cover and grabbed crusts of bread and discarded leftovers and crammed them into her mouth. Knowing her time was short, she grabbed as much as she could hold in her two hands and headed back to the closet. Then without considering the consequence, she turned toward her mother, swallowed the precious food, and asked a question.

"Why do you have those meetings?"

"What did you say?" her mother responded as she turned from loading the dishwasher, almost surprised to hear Dani ask a question.

Dani knew her curiosity would have a price.

"It is none of your business!" her mother yelled as she walked up to Dani. Dani turned to avoid the blow but her mother struck her on the back of her head sending her stumbling down the hall.

"It doesn't matter to someone like you. It isn't for you anyway. It never will be."

Struggling to keep her balance she was determined not to lose the morsels of food clutched in her hands even if she fell. Moments later she was back in the safety of the closet enjoying the last of her precious dinner from the trash.

During the time I had been helping Dani, she would bring me things. These things were usually items found in boxes in the garage that had been there since she had been married and had never been opened or sorted. Because of the feelings associated with each item, she would bring them to me to keep them for her.

I was seeing an increase in Dani's faith over our time together. She was finally making a break from the brainwashing and false teachings her father had filled her with over the years. As a result, she brought me items to keep for her that she knew she did not want to look at anymore. Most of the time, I would put them in my desk drawer and forget about them. One evening after all appointments were over and I was in the quiet solitude of the office, I felt prompted to open the drawer and explore the contents.

I was drawn to three items in the small stack of things she had given to me. Two sheets of paper folded separately and a small book that was obviously Scripture. I felt instantly that within these pages held some answers that would allow me to further help Dani. Most of what I had learned about her past so far had been very difficult, not just on me but particularly on her. I first reached for the folded piece of paper that looked to be the oldest.

As I gingerly opened the tri-folded piece of paper, I saw a date at the top and the heading *A Blessing given to Danielle Smith by her father.* The date was about a month after she was born. Obviously, someone had carefully recorded the blessing given to Dani with the best for her in health, education, and peace in her life. There were expressions of loving parents and a Heavenly Father who will be with her throughout her life. It was short but resonated a sweet, heartfelt sentiment from a tender father. I emitted a sigh of relief. One down . . . two to go.

The second paper was to prove far more interesting and ominous. I unfolded the twice folded paper and laid it in front of me. Across the top of the page it read *Patriarchal Blessing*. It was given to Dani around her fifteenth birthday and since this document is considered sacred in nature, I was about to fold it back up and put it away when I noticed some unusual things on the page. Some of the sentences had been blacked out and other words were hand written beside each. The margins on both sides had a line drawn from each of the hand-written words. These were obviously meant to change the meaning of the blessing.

"You will NEVER return to God."
"NEVER ever pray."
"Only I will direct you, not God."
"Only I can give you strength."
"You don't deserve blessings."
"Only I can give you counsel."
"The only work you can do is for me."
"You belong with me and no one else."
"You are evil and bad."

This was incredulous! I had difficulty accepting what I was seeing. How could anyone take a document intended to give hope, strength, and comfort and alter it in such a way? It also supported what Dani had been telling me about the memories she was starting to receive. There seemed to be a consistent pattern over the years to destroy Dani's hope, faith, and even her very trust in God.

I was starting to gain a new appreciation for what I was up against in trying to rescue Dani from abuse. Because it was becoming overwhelming, there was a moment of regret for having to take this burden with Dani. Then I was drawn to the third item which sat on my desk in a plastic bag.

I opened the bag and pulled out a small book of Scripture which was paper bound with crease marks on the exterior cover to indicate use and wear. By itself, it did not appear to be unusual or ominous. A flow of relief went head to toe as I determined that this book would be nothing unusual. I recalled that Dani had mentioned that this book was given to her by her father. It was the only set of Scriptures that she was allowed to have. In fact, she was told that if she wanted to read it she needed to have him there to read it with her.

I opened the cover and started turning the first few pages until I reached the table of contents. Several book titles which were delineated by chapters were totally crossed out. I observed that these books of Scripture had either teachings of the Savior or taught about forgiveness and God's love. At the bottom of the page in bold printed letters were the words:

NEVER READ

I slowly turned pages, one by one. What I saw shocked me. Whole paragraphs and even pages had been blacked out with a black marker. There was an amazing amount throughout the first book. I could almost imagine her father crossing things out and emphasizing that these parts didn't apply to her. I wondered, 'what was the purpose behind this?' My mind answered, 'To keep Dani from finding the truth.' Again, there was confirmation of an attempt by her father to suck the very life out of her.

In addition to this sacrilegious altering of sacred Scripture, I also notice words and phrases of text that were circled. These included words like *perish, evil, abominations, cast out, stoned, slain* and the list continued on in this negative theme. Obviously, the words were for specific emphasis. Lines were drawn from the circled phrases and words to the margins where, again, printed words had been added which altered and changed the meaning of the circled words. As in the other document, lines were drawn from the circled phases to the hand printed word *ME*. Later in the Scriptures, *ME* was changed to *DS*. I had to think for a minute and realized that these were Dani's initials. The message was clear, she was to understand these circled words of a negative and destructive nature were meant for her to internalize. I tried to imagine Dani reading this and being drawn constantly to the emphasized words. Reading words like *cast out, nothingness,* and *everlasting damnation* must surely have had an effect on her. Did she believe them? What effect did they have on her?

I continued to thumb through the rest of the book. Most of the pages were left untouched. Further into the book, some of the pages were completely folded over and some had the black marker blocking out complete chapters. Toward the end of the book I found a paragraph entreating people to repent and come unto Christ. This paragraph was crossed out and a line drawn to the added words: *THERE IS NO REPENTANCE FOR YOU.*

The bottom of the page was written in the same neatly printed manner and ended with: *YOU ARE CURSED!*

The closeness and quiet of the closet was comforting to Dani. As she listened she could hear the family having dinner, then clacking of dishes marked the end of the meal. Her father called the children into the living room. Although she knew she wasn't invited or wanted, she knew it was family night. She longed to sit with them, to sing songs and play games.

*"I am a child of God,
And he has sent me here."*

Although she wasn't there she mouthed the words to the song, careful not to make any noise. She rarely made that mistake anymore.

*"Has given me an earthly home,
With parents kind and dear."*

She could imagine them all sitting around the room, singing and having fun.

*"Lead me, guide me, walk beside me,
Help me find the way,*

*Teach me all that I must do,
To live with Him someday."*

Something always stirred within her when she heard these words. Peace? Comfort? She didn't know which nor did she even care. She just knew it was a good feeling.

After the lesson and activities, the house got quiet. She could tell her brothers and sisters were in bed. She was dozing off in the quiet and darkness when the door opened. She was instantly alert and tensed in preparation for a kick or a hit with the bat. To her surprise neither happened.

"Get out here now!" Her dad's voice was tense and strained but he kept the volume low probably so that he did not disturb the rest of the family. Dani scrambled to her feet and followed him down the hall to the living room.

"Sit," he said with a simple command.

In only her underwear she sat down on the floor near her father. Curiosity piqued her attention as this was certainly different from the usual routine. Without a word, her father put a piece of paper on the floor between them and began to write some words on the paper in two columns. He put her name at the top of the left column, and *God* at the top of the right column. On her side, he began to write words like stupid, worthless, insignificant, pitiful, demanding, whiny, fat, etc. Under the other column he put other words like perfect, kind, patient, loving, etc.

"Tonight, we sang *I Am a Child of God*. Are you a child of God?" her father asked.

Dani was afraid to answer but she nodded trying to guess what answer he wanted. In response, he smacked her on the side of her head.

"No, you aren't." he retorted. "You are NOT a child of God."

She looked up questioningly, half waiting for another blow. Instead he took his pen and pointed to the words under God.

"You see, God is all of these things. He is perfect and kind and loving. These are all things that you are not. So, you see you could never be a child of God." She looked down and he was pointing at the word *worthless*.

"God could never love someone like you. You are worthless to him, a throwaway. Because you are nothing like him, God doesn't want anything to do with you. He never will! Do you understand me?"

Dani looked up and nodded quickly in agreement.

"God doesn't ever listen to someone like you; so, don't even try. It is useless. Why would he listen to you? He doesn't even know who you are."

Tears started welling up in her eyes. She knew she could not let him see her tears so she exerted all her energies to control her emotions and her confusion.

"No matter what you do or how much good you could ever do, God will never change the way he feels about you. When you were in Heaven nobody wanted you, nobody! So, you were sent to our family and we are stuck with you." He emphasized the word *stuck* to make sure Dani heard it.

"You see, Danielle, nobody wants you. You don't belong anywhere."

Looking back over Dani's memories it was obvious that she had been systematically taught from a very early age that she was a throwaway, worthless to the world and even to God. Evil and insidious, this would be torture to an innocent mind and it would be very effective in preventing the abused victim from ever trusting someone and asking for help. With everyone being a potential danger, her father, no matter how bad the abuse was, would be her only security in life.

I carefully folded up the papers, put all the items in the bag, and then placed them back into the office drawer. I actually wanted to throw them away. At least these items would never ever hurt her again.

After Dani had arrived for our next session and had some time to relax and get settled, she began with a question.

"Why does God hate me?" she asked.

"He doesn't hate you, Dani." I responded.

"But God does hate me. He thinks I am worthless and a throwaway. I think I should just give up and go back." In her voice was resignation and defeat. I said a silent prayer and began.

"Dani, do you trust me?"

She nodded, barely looking up through the hair that had fallen over her face.

"Let me tell you about God, okay?"

Again, she nodded.

"God is our Father in Heaven - YOUR Father in Heaven. He is the great creator. He created the heavens and the earth. He created all the stars and worlds and people. In fact, His creations are so great that they cannot be numbered or understood." I paused to let her consider it. She had raised her head, pulled her blonde hair back and had given me her full attention.

I continued, "God is perfect in all things. It is only because he is perfect that he can ask us to be perfect. God created man in his own image. He gave us life. He presented a plan to us before we came here; we call it the Pre-Mortal Existence or pre-earth life. He gave us a choice to come to the earth and be tested, to see if we would obey his commandments. If we learned to obey his commandments then we could return to live with him again."

Dani's eyes were wide and trained on me. She was not only listening but she was understanding what I was teaching.

"Because God knew we would make mistakes, he provided a Savior for us who is Jesus Christ. He was to come to the earth, live a perfect live, suffer for our sins, and die for us. His power to rise from the grave allows us to be resurrected and his atonement allows us to be forgiven for our sins. He did this because he loves us, each and every one of us."

Again, I paused to see if she was going to ask any questions. She didn't, so I continued.

"You were told a lot of things about God growing up. Most of them were wrong. They were told to you so that someone could exercise power and control over you. Anyone that says anything more or less than what I have just told you is not of God. Anyone who pretends to be God is going to be accountable to God Himself. I would not like to be near the one that does that. God will not be mocked. I believe Him.

"Dani, you must believe that God is a God of miracles. He is perfect. He doesn't make mistakes. If He made mistakes He would cease to be God. That means YOU are NOT a mistake. You are not worthless. God knows who you are and knows everything about you. That also means you are not a throwaway. God does not make throwaways. Every one of His children is known to Him and is important to Him."

I stopped to give her a chance to think about what I had said. I looked across at Dani to see what effect this truth was having on her. To my surprise she had tears running down her cheeks. What an unusual and welcome display of emotion! I knew that she not only understood what I was telling her, but she felt the truth of it deep inside.

"So, God doesn't hate me?"

"No, Dani, He loves you."

"I am not a throwaway?"

"No, Dani, you are not a throwaway," I responded.

"And I am not cursed?" she asked as though she was waiting to be scolded.

"You are not cursed," I answered. "You never were."

More tears seemed to come. Then she looked at me and asked the question I was hoping would come.

"If God loves me, then why did He let me go through all . . .?" her voice faded out with a choke in her throat.

"I don't know how to answer that," I began. "God certainly knew what was happening to you. He gives men the ability to make choices and then they will be responsible for the consequences of their choices. When He does that, sometimes other innocent people get hurt."

"But, why didn't God protect me? Why didn't He rescue me?"

"I have thought about that a lot, Dani, because I knew that someday you would probably ask me that question. You went through abuse for most of your growing up years. Many of the things that happened to you were horrible and painful. But you had a remarkable way of burying the memory of each experience. Once those things happened and were over, you didn't have to deal with them anymore. That is why I think you survived and why you didn't just go crazy. THAT is one of the special gifts that I know that God gave to you. And to answer the question about rescuing you . . . He is rescuing you. He sent me to help you."

She sat pondering all that I said. She seemed to understand and it seemed to make sense to her, and much like a child she accepted it.

"Can you help me understand more?"

As we talked I had another idea come into my mind.

"Dani, I think I am going to add to the *New Rules* that I gave you. Is that okay?"

She nodded.

"Do you want a paper to write these down?" I asked while reaching for some paper and a pen.

"No need," she replied. "I will remember."

I gave her seven new rules. They would help her see herself as valued and empowered to take more control over her life. I started listing them and in her eyes, I could see her committing them to memory.

- *I am a daughter of my Heavenly Father who loves me and I love Him.*
- *I am in control of my life and I can make decisions.*
- *My body is a gift from God and I can make choices how my body should be treated.*
- *It is okay for me to disagree. My opinion counts.*
- *I don't have to believe everything everyone tells me. I can research, ask questions and learn on my own.*
- *No one deserves to be abused, ESPECIALLY ME!*
- *My top priority is to protect my kids and myself.*

At the end of the list she smiled. The tears streaming down her face were tears of joy. She looked to have a new lease on life. She sat straighter and taller. She appeared to have a new strength and confidence.

"Now I want you to study these new rules. Whenever you are feeling set upon by a trigger and hear those words telling you that you don't matter and that you are worthless, I want you to repeat these rules out loud so they become your new reality. Think you can do that?" I asked.

She nodded again. I could see that the chasm of hopelessness and worthlessness that her father had created for her was beginning to unravel. The control he had exerted over her for so many years was beginning to crumble, replaced with truths. I learned once more that God IS a God of miracles. With His help, I was able to help reverse a carefully planned program involving years of brainwashing and mind control methods. The wondrous majesty of God's power and glory which fills the universe descended for a brief moment to help one of

His struggling daughters in distress. I remembered a line from a classic movie called *The Ten Commandments*. In one scene Pharaoh, played by Yul Brenner, watches his Egyptian army as they are swallowed up by the Red Sea. The children of Israel had reached the other side safely and he had lost control of a whole nation of people forever. As he watched from his chariot, he uttered the words, "Their God IS God." Truer words were never spoken.

CHAPTER 15

An Unexpected Revelation

"Every picture tells a story, sometimes we don't like the ending. Sometimes we don't understand it."
–The Cheshire Cat
(Lewis Carroll, Alice in Wonderland)

The water was warm and soothing to the bruises she had received during a previous beating. The only sounds she could hear were the echoing drip of the faucet and her own breathing. With her eyes closed and the water above her ears she dreamed of playing in the yard, the warmth of the sun, and the feel of grass under her bare feet. She imagined her siblings liking her again and playing tag together, laughing, and running like they used to.

Suddenly, without warning, she felt pressure around her neck squeezing off her air supply. Her eyes opened wide in panic and she saw through the water her mother choking her and holding her under the water. She wildly tried to grab something with her hands and kick with her feet but to no avail. She could hear splashing water as she flailed her arms and legs.

Then she felt herself being lifted up out of the water. She tried to gulp for air. This failed as she was pushed under the water again. She struggled to hold her breath, to wait it out so she could breathe air again. Time had no meaning as this went on.

She remembered her mother's voice, calm and resolute. 'Why did you have to ruin everything? Why don't you just die?" It was like she had

An Unexpected Revelation

planned it or was carrying out a daily chore. Dani struggled for air and for control but she was just not strong enough. Her struggling exhausted every ounce of strength in her and then everything went black.

She had no idea how much time had elapsed. She just remembered waking up on the floor, naked and freezing. She choked and coughed up water and then took some welcome deep breaths. Then the memory faded in a dark cloud.

In Greek mythology, there is a story about a man named King Sisyphus who was the king of Ephyra (now known as Corinth). Because of his deceitfulness to the gods, he was condemned to roll a huge boulder up a steep hill. Each time he completed the task the boulder would roll back down to the bottom of the hill where King Sisyphus had to start all over again. I have always been fascinated by Greek mythology. Maybe that is why this story came to my mind when it did. It seemed that Dani was rolling this huge stone up a steep mountain. Each trigger and each memory started an uphill struggle trying to get past the brainwashing to the understanding of the realization that the triggers didn't need to be obeyed. Each time we would make a resolve to remember the new rules, the memories, like a giant boulder, would roll us back down to the bottom of our progression causing us to start over again.

Gratefully the memories seemed to slow down. It seemed to be linked to the announcement she made that she was pregnant. God in His mercy must have felt she didn't need to deal with both at once. Whatever the reason, I was glad because with a family and the pregnancy and everything else, I think she was about at her limit.

The cars that were following her car did not cease. She seemed to have one of three cars follow her from the time she would leave her house until she would arrive back home. They stopped parking in front of the house or down the street because I called the police and asked if they could be aware of some suspicious cars in the neighborhood. The local police must have responded because the cars took up position just outside of the subdivision and they waited there until she would drive by. I had her take different routes in and out of the neighborhood which threw off the effectiveness of their surveillance. Dani was getting really good at noticing when a car would start following her and she had perfected ways to lose them in traffic or in highly populated areas. I didn't know the significance of the different cars or who these other individuals were. I also didn't know yet the significance of the other police car that would show up occasionally and sit just out of camera range to watch the house. My big concern was that if the policeman was in partnership with her father that he might pull her over 'in the course of his duty' and then get to her. I had given Dani some instructions about that just in case. I told her under no circumstances was she to unlock the door or leave the car unless he (or she) called another local police officer to the scene.

"I can do that?" she had asked innocently.

"Yes!" I responded emphatically. "Of course, you can."

She was also still being harassed by her siblings. They continued to call and leave vile messages, accusing her of not being Christlike, ignoring her parents and being mean. These calls seemed to be escalating. Dani wouldn't listen to the messages but Jeff would tell her about them. They would also come to the door and pound and yell and insist she answer the door. The peephole that had been installed for her worked well and she didn't open the door, especially to someone that was going to chew her head off. This had been a difficult concept for her to understand but she managed to keep the door closed. She had been told what to do for so long she just thought that if she said 'no' to someone that it meant she was being mean.

"This is your house," I told her one day. "If you want to answer the door or the phone you can do it. If you don't want to it is still okay. And it is not mean. Do you understand?"

She nodded but I knew she was struggling with it.

"You are the parent. You need to do whatever is necessary to protect your children. If you keep an angry person out of your home so the children don't have to witness their lack of emotional control, then you can do it."

In time, Dani had a baby boy. Everything went well, no surprises at the hospital and mother and baby did quite well. Aside from the usual

An Unexpected Revelation

adjustment to the new little person in the house everything was going quite smoothly. Almost too smoothly. Even the surveillance cars backed away and the visits from angry family members stopped. Dani and her family started to enjoy a safe routine.

After the baby was several months old, the memories and triggers returned. She had been given a brief and yet needed vacation and now they had returned and were tougher and darker than before. It was like her subconscious was making up for the time off.

The space was cold and dark. The underside of the stairs could just barely be seen in the dim light. Dani could feel her heart racing. The small space gave little comfort as she had never before been this terrified. In an effort to provide both warmth and comfort, she huddled with her legs tucked to her chest in a hug.

She could still hear the screaming and yelling. Dani had been in her closet upstairs when the argument began. The references to *slut* and *whore* were obvious signs that she was the focus of their tirade. She had been called those names before many times. She had no idea what they meant but her guess was that they were not good. Whatever they meant, however, she knew that she deserved it. Her dad told her so.

It got quiet for a minute and then it started again.

"Put that gun away!" her mother yelled.

"I should have ended her years ago."

"Just put it away." This time the voice was a mixture of demand and pleading.

"Not yet," he responded.

Suddenly the closet door opened and Dani saw her father standing there with a gun in his hand. He reached in and grabbed her by the hair. She felt her body lift from the floor and then she was airborne. She bounced once on the bed and then ended up in a heap against the wall.

Suddenly there was an explosion as the gun went off. Whether by accident or on purpose, Dani had no idea. The sound was deafening in the small room leaving her ears ringing. Instinctively she put her hands over her ears and ran from the room. The closet beneath the stairs in the basement seemed to be the furthest and safest place she could find to hide.

She watched the underside of the stairs in anticipation of angry steps coming towards her. Slowly and deliberately the steps approached the door to the little closet under the stairs. Seconds later the door opened and a hand yanked her out into the open area in the basement. Goosebumps formed on her exposed skin.

She slowly looked up to see the barrel of the gun in her face. 'I hope he just kills me,' she thought. 'Then it would be over.' She tried to bravely face her father and the end.

"Why couldn't you have just gone away?" she heard her mother say from the top of the steps. "You are just ruining everything."

"I should have ended you a long time ago," her father spoke in a low determined voice. "You have been nothing but trouble."

Dani looked up the stairs to her mother for sympathy or help or something, but she was nowhere to be seen.

"You are worthless, understand? Worthless!" He paused for a moment looking at her then added, "You are only good for one thing."

She saw the gun start to lower and everything seemed to be absorbed in a dark mist and then the memory faded.

Dani was aware that she was dreaming and then she began to wake up. Through a haze she tried to make sense of what was happening. She was being held down and her dad was shaking her awake.

"Wake up, you worthless piece of garbage," he was saying.

As she opened her eyes for the third time she felt her mouth being forced open. "You need to take your medicine, open your mouth, damn you!" She fought hard to keep her mouth shut. She somehow knew what was going to happen. She tried to fight back but with her arms and legs held down she couldn't. So, she tried to keep her mouth shut.

"Damn you!" he rasped.

She felt a punch to her stomach which forced her breath out and her mouth to open. Her father poured some sort of liquid in before she could close it again. She tried to yell but he kept his hand over her mouth.

"Shut up or it will be worse for you," he said in a demanding tone. "If you know what's good for you, you won't make a sound."

An Unexpected Revelation

She continued to try to fight but something was happening. She was losing use of her arms and legs. She could see what was happening but she was powerless to respond.

Her father breathed a heavy sigh and stood up. He reached to undo his belt.

Even though Dani couldn't move, tears came out of her eyes in the only protest she could muster. At that point, the memory faded and dark mists took over.

I was amazed at the progress that Dani had made. She was finally making some progress in gaining control over the triggers and the memories. She needed less help on a regular basis and was doing things that most mothers do.

Our successes were sometimes short lived when a new batch of memories arrived. They brought with them horrible images as well as strong emotions. Rather than being full memories, they tended to be fragments which would cut off, ending abruptly. She instinctively knew that the rest of the memory must be really bad.

We continued to meet weekly when possible. During one of our sessions I allowed the conversation to progress as I allowed my thoughts to be guided by the Spirit. God knew her better than anyone and so I trusted that He would always help me. Our discussion went from family to her health issues and then to the memories. Then a thought occurred to me.

"When was the last time he abused you?" I asked referring to her father.

"Well, when I was carrying my last child. He would take his fist and punch me in the stomach and tell me that my kids would be no good and worthless just like me. He did that with each of my pregnancies." She paused as if in thought or trying to remember something.

"Didn't Jeff know?" I asked.

"No," she replied, "my dad pulled him aside just after we were married and told him that I had some serious problems and had been having them for years. He also told Jeff that he would step in and help out with the problems. So, my dad would come over all the time. I knew that if I said anything he would either hurt Jeff or my children. He said I was his and it didn't matter if I was married or not, I would never get away from him."

"So, he would come over after Jeff would leave for work. With the kids still sleeping he would hit me . . ." her voice trailed off, again as if in thought or trying to remember something.

After a few moments, she continued. "Yup, it has now been just over four years ago . . ." Again, her voice faded. Her face took on a faraway look for a minute or two and was replaced with a look of shock, fear, and realization at the same time.

"Oh my!" she exclaimed bringing her hands up to her face. "Oh my," she said again.

"You are remembering, aren't you?" I asked.

"He came over just ten months ago." She was taking shallow breaths now, her eyes in a faraway gaze as if she was watching it happening on a video monitor on the wall above my head.

"He had presents for the kids. He was alone and I didn't think anything of it." She was speaking in almost a whisper now. The color had drained from her face.

"Do you want to tell me more?" I asked.

"No wonder I don't like sleeping in my bed," she continued slowly. "He came in . . . he forced me into the bedroom . . ."

She looked devastated. Her eyes pleaded with me to make it all go away. I could see now that she was reliving it and suffering all over again; how he had taken her into the bedroom and forced her to have sex with him.

"I didn't remember. I am serious." It was like a platform had been pulled out from under her and she had lost her footing and was falling uncontrollably. "You have to believe me."

"I do, Dani," I said trying to comfort her. "I believe you."

"I didn't know. I didn't know," she was almost sobbing now. "I didn't remember."

"You buried this memory just like the others to protect you from something so horrifying that you couldn't cope with it otherwise."

"He is right, you know." She sounded defeated as if resigned to a fate that one could not avoid.

"Who is right?" I asked trying to gain a foothold to help her.

"My father," she said simply.

"In what way?"

"I am worthless and dirty and evil. I am everything he said I was." Her posture reflected resignation and defeat. "I am a throwaway. Now I know why God hates me!"

"You are not those things, Dani," I protested.

"Then why did God allow those things to happen to me? My dad told me that God didn't want me or even knew I existed. I believe him now."

It was obvious now that the beatings were his way of exhausting her into submission allowing him to sexually abuse her without resistance. I could not begin to comprehend all that this girl had been through. But I knew that God knew and understood her completely and now I had to help her understand that truth.

"Well, I know one thing for sure, Dani," I responded thoughtfully.

Looking at me with a glimmer of hope in her eyes she responded, "What is that?" Her voice still reflected sadness.

"Remember what I told you about God? God is perfect. He created this whole earth and all the stars in the heaven. He is so amazing that His creations go down to the size of a neutron or proton or even smaller and all these things work in beautiful and perfect harmony. So, if God created all these things, you have to realize He created each of us. Remember? God does not make mistakes. He is perfect and His creations are perfect."

I hoped that she would remember our prior discussion about God. I paused to see if she was understanding this concept, then I continued.

"You, Dani, are one of His creations. And because you are one of His creations I know that He loves you."

"But how can you know? How?" she pleaded.

"Before I answer that, let me ask you a question, okay?"

She nodded.

"Most of the time that you were growing up, you lived in a closet or a garage or a cupboard. Why do you think he did that?"

"To hide me because nobody wanted me," she answered as if to say I told you so.

"I disagree. He certainly was trying to hide something. He really did it to hide what he was doing from the world. He didn't want anyone to know what he was doing to you during all those years. After a while he couldn't take the chance that you might tell someone so that everyone would find out. His reputation, his job, his family were all on the line and if someone found out, it would mean prison or worse for him."

Dani was thinking about that. She seemed to be understanding, so I kept going.

"His intention was to keep you hidden in a closet for the rest of your life. You told me that he said you were his and you would never be free from him, right? He never planned that you would get married. He saw you only as his property and under his control."

Again, she nodded.

"He had no intention of letting you go. He told you those things about God and being worthless so that you wouldn't ever try to leave him. What he did was cruel and sick and against everything that God teaches and stands for. Each of His creations are precious to Him. Before you came here you were a perfect and precious spirit daughter. You are still His perfect and precious daughter inside."

She was sitting up more and leaning forward in her chair listening to every word. I was grateful that the words were being given to me as I was speaking. I knew it was a message from a Father to a daughter.

"So here is how I know that God loves you and that you are amazingly special to Him."

She was wiping the tears from her face, now having some color returning to it. She was truly absorbing the inspired words and her spirit was transforming as they filled her soul. Dani was truly understanding that she was valuable, needed, and special. Without waiting for a response, I continued.

I opened my drawer and pulled out a picture of her children that she had given me several months previous. I set it on the desk, rotated it 180 degrees and slid it over for her to see clearly.

An Unexpected Revelation

"This is why. Would a cruel God that hated you and thought you were worthless and a throwaway give you such precious little gifts for you to take care of?"

Suddenly a light turned on in her eyes, showing comprehension and understanding previously lacking in her life. She was connecting God to the miracles that were her children.

"If your dad had his way, you would never have had these children. He tried to prevent it by hitting you in the stomach when you were pregnant. He has tried brainwashing, threats, and beatings. And in spite of all of this, God has been able to get you out of abuse and has given you beautiful children and a loving husband. The only type of God that would allow that to happen would be a kind and loving God. If He thought you were worthless and hated you, would He have gotten you out of abuse and allowed you to have children?"

There didn't need to be an answer to the question. I could tell by her expression that it was making sense to her. She loved her children and knew that it was really a miracle that she had them.

"Is that why God provided you?" she asked innocently. "To teach me and help me understand these things?"

I had never really thought of it that way. "I am sure you are right. I am sure God brought us together for a reason."

"There is another thing I know as well," I added.

"What is that?" she asked.

"I know that no matter what someone can do to your body or to mine, that inside our bodies our spirits stays intact. Our spirits stays pure and clean."

"What do you mean? Can you explain it more?"

"When you were being abused and all those terrible things were happening to you, who chose to do those things to you?"

With eyebrows knit with questioning she replied, "My father."

"Did you choose to have those things done to you?"

"No," she replied.

"So, you didn't choose to be beat or raped or kept in a closet or yelled at?"

"No, I didn't choose any of those things."

"Then you are not responsible for what happened to you. Your father is. He will have to account for all those things that happened to you for all those years. You were the victim. He lied to you, brainwashed you, and abused you. He made the decision, and took your ability to decide away from you. The reason you had your things taken away, were kept in a closet, and beaten was so that he could control you in every way, denying you any ability to make your own decisions."

Dani's eyes were wide with a hint of sadness reflected in them. Probably, for the first time in her thirty years of life, she was being told that something was NOT her fault, and that she was NOT responsible for all the things that had happened. A huge weight was being lifted off her shoulders. She was beginning to feel value as a child of God.

She started to cry tears of joy. She was recognizing that the things she was taught her entire young life were wrong. She was building a new foundation that would give her a life of peace with a sure promise of God's love, full of hope and meaning.

I sat back with a sigh of relief and silently thanked my Heavenly Father for helping to give a life of freedom back to one of His choice daughters. This really was a miracle.

Dani looked up at me and with all the sincerity and gratitude of a rescued soul, said, "You see me like Jesus and Heavenly Father see me, don't you?"

"I have always seen you as a young woman, a daughter of God," I replied.

"Thank you for seeing me as something other than broken. Thank you."

After our session, I had to take some time to think. As usual I walked into the chapel. Since nobody was in the building I left the lights off and walked up to the back row of the choir seats and sat down. I felt peace there, and I needed peace right then.

I was struggling inside with the pure evil and wickedness of Dani's father. He had spent his whole life being two people, a human chameleon of sorts. To everyone around him, he was an upstanding father, husband, and church member. He accepted callings in his church and performed them. Dani had told me that she remembered some of them over the years and they held meetings in their home. From her vantage point in a

An Unexpected Revelation

closet she could hear much of what went on. She would hear them talk of compassion and caring and loving your neighbor. He appeared to be above reproach to neighbors and other church members.

He had created such a fabricated story regarding Dani that everyone believed her to be mentally unstable. Even after she came home from the psych ward, she was given prescribed medication to control psychotic episodes that had never existed. The meds made her lethargic, sleepy, and spacy. These results would let her father keep her controlled and submissive. To the outside world, she looked the part of the crazy child and even her siblings believed that to be the truth.

From what I could conclude from her memories, the drugs worked very well. They kept her under control and gave her the appearance of being unstable. The facade worked extremely well. Over time both family members and neighbors were convinced she was unstable: a danger to herself and possibly to others. This must have been a dream come true for her father because even if she did tell someone what he was doing to her, nobody would believe her.

The saddest truth is that nobody did believe her for most of her life.

CHAPTER 16

Why Can't They Stop?

"When you save a girl, you save Generations."
—Mary N. Cook, 1st Counselor. YW
General Presidency, LDS Church.

Dani awoke naked and curled in a fetal position on a concrete floor. As she opened her eyes she could tell it was midday. Sunlight streamed in through both broken and unbroken glass panes. The area she was in was huge. It was the largest garage she had ever been in. This place had an echo-like quality and was empty except for some huge pieces of machinery and some doorways at one side that led to some offices or rooms. She looked around and realized she was alone. How long she had been there she didn't know. Not only did she not know but she didn't care.

She only knew she felt sick and hurt. She was also afraid. Her stomach ached and had sharp pains. She was afraid because she didn't know what was happening to her. Sometimes she was cold and shivering violently and at other moments she would sweat.

Her stomach now large and extended would cramp up so hard it brought tears to her eyes. At times, she could hear her screams echo against the distant walls and high ceiling of the building. After each scream, she half expected someone to come out and yell at her for being so loud, but nobody came. Instinctively she felt her breathing come in short panting bursts as another cramp came. As the cramp got worse her stomach got hard as a rock, then the cramping would subside and she would lay there exhausted.

She asked herself why this was happening and why nobody was there helping her. In her fifteen years of life, she had never experienced anything like this. She longed for her mother and to be held, comforted, and loved but she hadn't seen her mother for weeks, maybe months. She couldn't say how long because she had lost all track of time.

The cramps were hurting more, with greater intensity and they were coming closer together. Each cramp lasted longer and came with greater intensity. Tears rolled down her cheeks. Dani was becoming more and more convinced that whatever it was that she had, she was going to die from it. A quick end would be a tender mercy to what she was experiencing. If only God could hear her thoughts and take her soon. The pain and cramping had been going on for hours with no end in sight.

Suddenly the cramp started with such intensity and gave her an urge to put her head to her knees. Why? Fear and panic rose up within her.

"Help me!" she yelled as best she could. She cried through the pain and the cramps. An extremely strong cramp grabbed her and she found herself halfway lying on her back while simultaneously trying to sit up until the cramping subsided.

"I need help," she yelled again. There was still no response. "I don't know what is happening to me." The last of her words were choked with a massive cramp and another urge to sit up. She suddenly felt the fear leave and felt a blanket of comfort rest on her. It almost felt as though she wasn't alone anymore.

With each need to push herself up, she felt movement then there was one final push and a scream that echoed around the building. She fell on her back and breathed deep breaths exhausted. The pain of the cramps was replaced with a different kind of pain but compared to what she had just experienced, it was much less in comparison. She lay there trying to catch her breath and regain some strength for several minutes before she became aware of a noise and some movement. On the floor between her legs was a baby. Instinctively she wanted to pick it up and hold it, but she was too exhausted.

Then she was aware of another presence. She turned her head to see two men walking up, one was her father and the other man she didn't recognize. Her father gestured to the other man who knelt down and picked up the baby.

"Please," Dani pleaded, "let me hold her." She tried to get up but couldn't get her body to work.

With no emotion, the man sneered at Dani, nodded in agreement with her father and then turned on his heel and walked away. With every fiber of her being she tried to get up, to get to the baby, her baby. She craved to hold it and cradle it in her arms. As she tried, exhaustion overcame her. Once more she lay back, tears streaming from her eyes and then darkness overcame her and she lost consciousness.

I had received a call from Dani regarding a memory. She had described it as the worst memory that she had ever had and needed help in understanding it. She shared the memory with tear-filled eyes and a terrible ache in her heart. It was now clear to her why she had been so afraid of childbirth after she got married and why she felt a great and heavy loss in her life.

I had not expected anything like this. As usual, she not only had remembered the memory but the associated fear, pain, and loneliness that came with the memory. She was now realizing that she had another child out there . . . somewhere. Together we talked about God's love and mercy. We also discussed that God knew the beginning from the end and that I truly felt that God would make it right with her someday.

My biggest fear was that Dani might become angry or bitter toward her father for the events that had happened to her. It would not be surprising at all for Dani to think that life had been horribly unkind to her. For her to harbor thoughts of revenge or hatred would not be surprising.

Amazingly I never saw any of this with Dani. Occasionally, I wondered if she was just a time bomb waiting to go off. But time proved how amazing she really was. Not once did I ever see any anger or hatred come out in any form. She didn't hate her dad and she thought if she could talk to him that maybe she could mend their relationship. I strongly recommended against that given his propensity for violent behavior. However, she seemed to have acquired a far greater depth of forgiveness and love than I could have imagined possible considering all she had experienced at his hands.

This memory caused me to really struggle. Just imagining Dani there on the concrete floor in labor alone caused me great mental anguish. During this time, I even wondered why God had not come to her rescue sooner. I couldn't get it out of my mind. It was then I remembered another woman, possibly a teenager, who had delivered a baby in lowly circumstances, in a manger, but at least she was not alone. She had a husband that cared for her and most likely a midwife. I couldn't reconcile the fact that Dani had been alone, a teenager, without help. Dani not only experienced having her first child alone, she also had her child taken from her.

In the early hours later that morning, I found myself kneeling in a quiet place in my home. Only the tick of the clock and an occasional creak of the house settling could be heard. I poured my heart out to God in part for Dani because of the injustice she had endured. I could not feel consoled as I prayed. I wept as I pleaded to somehow understand the *whys*.

After a time, I felt peace come to me. In my mind, I could see Dani alone once more in that building on the concrete in labor. This time I could see that she was not alone. In my mind, I could see several individuals dressed in white ministering to her, telling her what to do and giving her comfort. Then a Scripture came to my mind from the words of the Savior from the book of Matthew:

Are not two sparrows sold for a farthing?
and one of them shall not fall on the ground without your
Father. But the very hairs of your head are all numbered.
Fear ye not therefore, ye are of more
value than many sparrows.
—Matthew 10:29-31 KJV

I felt reassured and strengthened that God was in charge and it wasn't for me to know everything. That night I found comfort and peace. It was sufficient for me to understand that God knew what happened and He will make it right with Dani and hand out justice His way and in His time. I also learned that God knew what happened to Dani in that building that day and He showed His love even to this little fallen sparrow.

"You are too fat!"

The volume of the words made an echo in the small bedroom. These words yelled by Dani's father used to hurt. Now they let her know that no matter how much she tried to lose weight, she failed to meet her dad's expectation.

Standing against the wall dressed only in her underwear, Dani felt him pinch what she perceived was a roll of fat on her side and around her stomach. She only knew that she was fat and her father was displeased. As Dani looked down at the fingers pinching her, she didn't notice the bones of her ribcage pushing the skin out in a skin-over-skeleton manner. She didn't see her pronounced hip bones underneath her thin underwear. All she knew was that she was eating too much and that she was too fat. She knew she had to do something about that to make her father happy. If she could just get the fat gone maybe he would treat her like he did the other children. Maybe life would return back to the way it was before . . . before he started hurting her.

"You understand?" he shouted. "You are just too fat. Are you sneaking food?"

She shook her head. She hadn't been sneaking food, there were punishments for that. She had hardly eaten in days. Her young mind could not comprehend how she could gain weight and not eat. If he said it was true, it must be so. She determined to somehow eat less.

"You are so worthless! If I catch you sneaking food you know what will happen, right?"

She nodded this time looking at the floor.

"If you continue to be fat I will have to get rid of you. I can't believe how fat and lazy you look. Nobody likes fat girls, not even God."

As Dani looked at the floor trying not to make eye contact she didn't notice him approaching. The first indication was a punch to the stomach which took her breath away. As he hit her, she believed that she deserved it because she was fat and lazy. That is what happens when you are fat and lazy, you get punished. After the beating she knew what was coming next. She was too tired to fight him or resist. She just let it happen. Letting it happen did not stop the tears that streamed down the side of her face.

Then the memory faded in swirls of black mists. Dani realized that she had just experienced another memory, however, in her mind it was so real she could not tell the difference between the memory and the present. She was confused and frightened. She felt dirty and unclean. The one thought that dominated the rest, directed her next action. She walked into the kitchen and making sure the kids were not looking, she opened the lid to the trash and picked out a couple pieces of stale bread crusts and quickly ate them before anyone noticed.

She was devastated in the weeks following the realization that her father had been sexually abusing her. She saw herself as unclean and dirty. We had several discussions about the fact that God did not think she was fat and that He would love her anyway even if she was. But she couldn't get it out of her mind that she needed to please her father and lose weight.

"When he comes to get me, I don't want to be fat," she would tell me.

"But you are not fat. Trust me," I said thinking of my increasing middle. "I understand fat."

"His voice is loud in my head. He says that I am fat and I have to believe him."

"He is not here, how can he tell you what to do?" I asked.

"It's in my head, silly," she said as if I should already know the answer. "I can hear his voice and I need to obey it."

"What do you mean, *when he comes to get you?*" I asked.

"That is his voice, too. He always said that I can never get away from him and he will always find me and that I can never get away."

"But you did get away, remember?" I responded.

"He'll come back. He'll find me."

I was getting frustrated. I was not frustrated at Dani but at the man who had caused so much pain and conflict in her mind that she couldn't tell the difference between memory and reality. The recent realization of sexual abuse had caused a major setback in Dani's progress. She came wearing jeans and a long-sleeve shirt like she usually did, but this time it was more obvious than ever that she was losing weight. She was too thin, the 'skin and bones' thing once more. My frustration changed to worry. Even the new rules appeared to have been circumvented. She was going to kill herself by not eating so she could please a dad who abused her and whom she hadn't seen in over a year. It didn't make sense to me but somehow to her it did. I knew if he knocked on her door right now she would go with him. I had to do something to prevent that from happening.

"Dani, you are experiencing the triggers that have been brought back by these new memories. Those voices inside your head are only memories, they are not your dad speaking to you. Understand?" We had these conversations before. I had come to realize that the new rules needed to be repeated and constantly reinforced.

She looked at me quizzically for a minute and then shook her head. "The voice is so loud, it drowns out everything else. It is telling me that I am fat and worthless and dirty."

"They are only memories," I replied emphatically. "They are not happening now. You have not spoken to your dad in over a year now. He is not and cannot be saying those things. You have to understand that they are just memories." I was hoping that I was getting through to her.

"But I am fat. Just look at me." She was desperately trying to get me to see the sense of what her mind was telling her.

"Would you do something for me?" I asked.

She looked at me for a minute.

"Do you trust me?" I asked hoping that I knew the answer.

She tried to smile and said, "Yes, I do. What do you want me to do?"

"Pull your shirt sleeve up on your arm, please."

She unbuttoned the cuff and pulled the sleeve up above her elbow. Her arm was alarmingly skin and bones. There was very little muscle. How could she still be a walking, functioning human being? I didn't need to see the rest of her body to know that she had been starving herself.

"Look at your arm, Dani. There is no fat there, you are not fat." I wanted her to come back to reality. I needed her to see her body as it really was.

"What do you mean? His voice is telling me I am fat." When she said it this time she didn't sound so sure.

"I mean that in order to be fat you have to have fat showing under the skin. What is under the skin on your arm?"

She thought for a minute trying to register what I was saying and what she was believing. She finally said, "Just my bones."

"That is right. Just your bones. At the rate you are going, they are going to have to admit you into the hospital."

"But," she tried to hang onto the memories, "he says I am fat."

"Can I ask you more questions?" Over the period of time I had been working with her, showing her respect and offering her the option to say 'yes' or 'no' had given her empowerment over her life and her thinking. This was a freedom she had never enjoyed nor been given by her parents. She nodded.

"How do you feel right now?"

She seemed to be doing an internal assessment. "I am really tired and weak."

"If it wasn't because you were fat, why else would your father want you to stop eating?"

She looked at me blankly, not recognizing that there could be any other reason. It had been drilled into her mind so deeply that she had accepted it as absolute truth.

I continued, "If you were weak and lethargic you couldn't fight back, you couldn't run, and you couldn't escape. You would be too weak to even attempt it. Your thinking would be blurred and you would start to even question yourself. That way he would have complete control over you."

She felt her arms and her stomach and ribs beneath her shirt. There was a puzzled look on her face.

"You mean I am not fat?" she asked.

"No, you are not fat," I replied.

"You mean his voice in my head is just a memory?"

I nodded this time.

Tears started forming in her eyes. Her facial features changed to one of questioning. "Why would he do such a thing?" she asked. "Why?"

"I don't know why, Dani," I replied. "But together we are going to make sure he doesn't ever do it again."

She agreed and decided she should go home and try to eat. She had made a major step in overcoming the powerful memories and triggers. Although this was not a final victory, I knew we had made a huge run towards the marathon finish line. Finally, she was gaining power in her life once again, seeing the memories and her father for what they really were. Before she left I reinforced the importance of the new rules. She promised to review them several times a day.

Gradually Dani started gaining some weight. There were times she would call and ask me why she thought she still looked fat. When she started eating again, her body rejected the food. She would eat a meal and then she would go into the bathroom and throw it up. Maybe it was due to some sort of conditioning that was in place to control her weight. If she ate, she could throw it up and thereby control her weight herself. It was very possible that in her mind, with all the control taken away by her father, that this was the only control she could maintain that he could not influence. The words from the movie, *What About Bob* (Oz, 1991), came to me: Baby Steps. So, I used that idea to help her with eating again. I suggested that instead of large meals a few times a day that she should eat many small ones or even just small bites and swallow them, wait and try it again. Amazingly, it worked. After a while she did not have a desire to throw up and within a few weeks she had gained enough weight so that she did not look so emaciated.

When I was a young boy I remember seeing a book in my house. I don't know where it came from or why we had it, but later I realized it was a copy of *Dante's Inferno*. I later learned that the word *inferno* was

Italian for Hell. I remember leafing through the pages, not really reading the words but just viewing the pictures. Ornate drawings depicted people, lots of people, half dressed and crowded in a small area. Some were laughing at other people while some had the appearance of being tortured or in pain. In the background behind the people were fiery flames that rose up without seeming to have a source. A couple of people appeared to be trying to escape this inferno. One individual, taller than the rest, with the appearance of being in charge, was extending a whip out to the escapees and he was laughing as the whip encircled them around the waist preventing them from leaving Hell.

I don't remember much else about the book. I don't think I even read any of the contents. What I did remember was the feeling I had watching the devil have his way with these poor souls. I had no idea what they had done, or if they even deserved being in Hell. I felt bad for those souls who appeared to be doomed to live forever under the control of the devil himself. Above all of this I did remember being scared with the realization that once Satan has some control over an individual, he not only rejoices in that control but he never gives it up.

That is what I was feeling about Dani and her father. Together we had worked so hard to help her realize that she had control and that she was not under her dad's control any more. She also had the ability to make decisions that would control her own life and her own destiny. That is the exact opposite from the life her dad had chosen for her. He had tried his best to circumvent her agency and take it completely away from her. Now circumstances kept arising which gave me the impression that the devil himself was at work to keep control over Dani.

About a month or so later the memories were still coming, but by now Dani was using some personal tools and strength to manage them much better without the former devastating and debilitating effects. I was starting to feel better about her condition and was enjoying a brief rest from the intense concern that had become an almost constant in my duty as her bishop. Then I received a call from Dani.

"Jeff didn't show up for work today. I am worried." There was a touch of panic in her voice.

"I am sure you tried to call him on the phone. What did he say?" I asked casually.

"He didn't answer. It went right to voice mail," she responded.

"Has this ever happened before?" I asked searching for a reasonable explanation.

"No. He runs his schedule like clockwork. He just doesn't miss work." The more she talked, the more worried she sounded.

"Has he had any change in behavior or has anything changed to upset him?"

There was a pause at the other end of the phone. "There was something," she replied.

"What was that?" I asked.

"He completely lost his temper a day or so ago. He was throwing things and punched a hole in the wall. The kids were scared and ran to their rooms to hide."

"What do you think caused that?" This incident had to be related.

"I noticed that he had run out of his medication. He said that he was doing well and didn't need it anymore. He was tired of taking the meds and felt that he could control his condition now."

"What is he taking the medication for?"

"I don't know if I ever told you but Jeff is bipolar," she responded. "I didn't think too much of it."

Limited experience had taught me that if Jeff didn't take his medication with this condition that he could experience dramatic mood swings. He might seem normal and happy one minute and then the exact opposite within the next minute. This sudden outburst of anger was a good indicator that he was off his medication.

"What should I do?" she asked.

"Well, first, see if you can get his medication refilled, okay?" I asked.

"Okay. What else?"

"Keep calling his phone and see if you can reach him. You might call his doctor and let him know as well. He could be a danger to himself as well as others." I continued. "If he calls, try to locate where he is so you can get his medication to him."

"Anything else?" she asked.

I thought for a moment and an idea came to me. "Dani? Do the kids have backpacks?" I asked.

"Yes, why?"

"I just have an idea and I want you to trust me on this. Just pack a set of extra clothes for each of the kids, underwear, toothbrush, and a toy and then put the backpacks in the very back part of your van. Understand?"

Without hesitation she replied, "Okay," and hung up the phone.

Several hours later I was at home with my family. It was after the kids were in bed and the house was quiet. My wife and I had talked about some of our plans for the future, the state of our finances, and a couple of repairs that were needed around the house. We were just heading to bed when I receive a text from Dani.

"I heard from Jeff. He was crying on the phone. He said my dad called him and told him I was doing men in the house during the day while he was at work. He said he isn't coming home anymore. I QUIT!"

CHAPTER 17

Clouds of Darkness Gather

*Come unto me, all ye that labour
and are heavy laden, and I will give you rest.
²Take my yoke upon you, and learn of me;
for I am meek and lowly in heart:
and ye shall find rest unto your souls.
For my yoke is easy, and my burden is light.*
—Matthew 11:28-30 KJV

I am convinced of an all-knowing and loving God who dwells in the Heavens and desires to help His children. He is a God who knows all things from the beginning to the end. I have sometimes wished, however, to have a little bit more advanced warning of what was going to happen. It would be extremely helpful in our life's critical moments. It is possible that we cannot be trusted with too much of that advanced information because we might misuse it. Even so, I am grateful that He has blessed me with what I needed at the moment I needed it, when I have been focused on doing the right things. I knew at this moment Dani and her little family also needed His help.

Fueled by a lie, Jeff had been convinced that his wife was unfaithful. For a man who adored his wife, it would be devastating news even if it were not true. It now appeared that her father had orchestrated an event with the intent of leaving Dani alone without a husband and protector. With that vulnerability, she would certainly be easier prey. Now he would just need to pick the time and there would be little resistance. He was going to be true to his promise that Dani would never get rid of him and she would always be his.

If her dad and I were picking sides, just like we did while playing kickball in school, he appeared to have the lion's share of excellent team players on his side. He had turned her mother as well as brothers and sisters against her by making them think she was crazy and unstable. Now he had turned her husband against her with a vicious lie, causing him to stop taking his medications with the result being a bipolar episode. Our two teams seemed tremendously unbalanced.

How could I have foreseen any of this? Even without the benefit of knowing what the future was going to bring, I trusted in God that He would not abandon this little family. Surely, He would not allow all the work that had been done to help Dani get out of abuse to be lost. Did not God, as a trial, almost allow Abraham to sacrifice his only son on an altar before stopping him at the last minute in a test of faith and obedience? Abraham did not doubt God and at this moment neither could I doubt God.

While speaking with Dani, I shared with her some of my thoughts. Even though things appeared dark now, I believed everything would be alright. I also assured her that she now had the strength to meet these challenges just fine. With these assurances, she went about taking care of children and trying to locate her husband and get his medications to him.

I also discussed the need, more than ever, to follow the new rules. Her first priority was to protect her children and herself and not let anyone into the house that she did not trust.

About mid-morning she called me concerned. "I was on the internet and checking our accounts and most of our money is all gone."

"What do you mean *all gone*?" I asked.

"Almost all the money in all our accounts except one has been drained. Jeff said something last night about buying things, but he wasn't making sense."

"So, you said you had money in one account, right?"

"Some, but not much."

"This morning, go down to the bank and take out what you can before it disappears as well. That will give you something to live on until we get Jeff stabilized again with his medication. Were you able to reach his doctor?"

"Yes, he returned my call this morning. He confirmed that his behavior is consistent with failing to take his medicine. I am going to pick up his refill this morning."

"Well done, Dani. See? You are managing, aren't you?" I asked, giving her some support.

"Yes, thank you," she replied. The call ended.

Even with this immediate crisis, the memories did not stop for her. The worst of the worst were still coming. With the knowledge now that she had been sexually abused by her father, it seemed that all the associated memories with that kind of abuse were coming. At times, she was overwhelmed. I suggested that she write them down in an effort for her to quickly resolve these while still taking on her present challenges. Even with the continuing flash memories, Dani was amazingly calm. She had a list of things to do and accomplish which helped keep her focus on the important task of family.

That evening I called her to get an update. When she answered I could tell that she was in her car.

"Where are you?" I asked concerned.

"In a parking lot near Costco," she replied calmly.

"What are you doing there?" I asked incredulously. I was concerned about her being setup and being abducted by her father and she was calmly sitting in a parking lot.

"Don't worry, I am safe," she replied calmly. "Jeff called. He needed some clothes and some money so I gave him what he needed. He looked horrible, like he hadn't slept in days."

"But what about the kids? Are they with you?"

"No, silly," she replied with a chuckle. "I asked a neighbor friend of mine to watch the kids for me. She has strict instructions not to let anybody in."

I let out a sigh of relief. I was amazed that she was in the middle of the city, twenty minutes driving time on the freeway and meeting Jeff. But she was safe and the kids were safe.

"I did give Jeff his meds. There is no telling how long he has been off them. He promised to start taking them again."

"Did he indicate where he had been and what he has been doing?" I asked trying to make some more sense of all this.

"He was crying one minute and angry the next. I honestly don't think he remembers what has happened and where he has been." She was still amazingly calm and in control. "I also made him promise to call his doctor. I don't think he will remember that part though."

"Where is he now?" I asked, still concerned about her safety.

"I am watching him walk away with his clothes and a blanket I gave him. I don't know where he is going, but I did what I could for him."

Her compassionate side demonstrated the type of woman she had become and probably always had been. She was willing to put herself in danger to help someone she knew needed help and it didn't matter if he was unstable or possibly dangerous. This was the Dani that had been buried all these years and that God was bringing back.

"So, what are you going to do now?" I asked.

"I need to get back home to my children," she replied still sounding in control.

"Be safe and watch for anyone following you, okay?" I admonished.

"Don't worry. I remember ALL the rules." The line went dead again for the second time that day and I had a peaceful feeling that she would be safe and was doing just fine.

During this current crisis with Jeff, the memories still kept coming. Over the next several days I received the following emails:

I feel dirty, and so disgusting, like trash. The memory from last night is more than I can handle. It was so overwhelming. I know you say I can do it, but today I don't think I can. I don't feel confident in anything.

I know you probably won't see this email today, but I need to write. Otherwise I will do something I really know I shouldn't. Church was hard today. So much information, so many conflicting memories. I ended up in Primary with one of my kids who was struggling. I had a memory come when they started singing 'If the Savior Stood Beside

Me'. (I can't do this, I am not tough enough or strong or anything like that. I don't feel confident. I feel very blue.) I was watching the little children sing that song and I remembered being in Primary when I was young. I remembered the smell, the look of the primary room and the feel of the place. I even remembered the feel of the wood on my hands. I remembered feeling so dirty and hurting from what happened the night before. I felt embarrassed and out of place. I remember feeling that I didn't belong. I remember feeling for the first time distant from the Savior. I really thought he hated me and that he thought I was as dirty and disgusting as my dad said I was.

I was thinking about all the Sundays, with all the talks and lessons that my father sat through or gave. Ten years is a very long time to hide this 'secret' isn't it? In those ten years and the hundreds of times that he did it, and the hundreds of things he said, twelve times of being stitched up because of his cutting me, throwing up more times than I can count, being drugged more times than I can count, and so many visits to the hospital . . . and no one noticed! No one stopped it and no one helped. That doesn't make what he did right, does it? Or anything I did wrong, does it? It still isn't my fault . . . right?

I think I understand what you have been trying to tell me. I now see what I was trying to do. I get a little confused because of being told so many times that I was doing it because I was crazy. They would say I wanted attention but instead of listening they would put me on medicine. I am starting to understand the real reasons behind a lot of what happened. So, you were saying that I was using my body to say things that verbally I could not. Why didn't anybody notice? When I send my kids to school I can't imagine them cutting themselves and no one questioning it. I can't imagine them starving themselves or throwing up and no one questioning it. Does that make sense? I understand when you say that the eating disorder and the cutting were the only things that I could control. Is that why he put me in the hospital so many times and put me on medications – because HE couldn't control the behavior? He needed to keep his secret. Does that make sense?

In my memory, he says he does it just for me. He says that I am special because I am the only one. When I have the nightmares, I can hear him saying that. I can hear him saying that I am different and that is why he loves me so much. He says that I am different from the other girls. What does that mean? He says that I am different and special because I am not like my mother. I don't understand. Does that mean I am not any good now? What is special love? What does he mean?

I want to cut so badly. I can't throw up because there is nothing there to throw up. I feel so blue.

During the intervening days, Jeff became more stabilized but he still refused to come home. He had decided to stay with his father for a while. Dani could tell that the real Jeff she had married and loved was not quite back to his normal self yet. It hurt Dani a lot that he did not want to come home but she didn't really show the hurt when we spoke.

Jeff's doctor had called him to make sure he was not a danger to anyone and reassured Dani that it would be several days before the medications would take effect given the fact that they had no idea when he stopped taking them.

Dani received an increased number of phone calls from her father and siblings trying to get her to visit them or allow them to come over. When she asked my opinion in the matter I tried to let Dani make her own decision. I asked if she really wanted to have contact with them. The painful memories were too fresh for her to feel up to it. When their coaxing over the phone didn't work they started pounding on her door, yelling that she was not Christlike and she was hurting the whole family. The messages on the phone were becoming worse and even included profanity. Eventually, she quit listening to the messages all together.

Dani didn't feel it was safe to even leave the house. After she had pulled the money out of the bank she stocked up on food and staples for the kids. She felt that someone was watching the house but couldn't see anyone. Occasionally I drove by the house just to make sure that it looked safe and no lingering, suspicious people were hanging around.

It almost felt like a huge storm was approaching and I found myself praying and hoping that we were prepared enough for what was ahead.

It was late the next day that Dani called with some interesting news.

"Jeff called. He said my father had contacted his dad and had called a family meeting," she began. She was very calm and emotionally detached.

"What does that mean, a family meeting?" I asked.

"I don't know. Jeff said that he and his dad were invited along with my family. He did say that I was not invited."

"I find that really weird. I have never really heard of a family meeting that includes both sides of the family and does not include some sort of wedding or death or something." I was trying to figure out what was going on and what her dad was up to. "Did Jeff say anything else?"

"No, just that I wasn't invited. He didn't know much else." She paused for a minute considering and then added, "What do you think is going on?"

"I just don't know. Maybe your dad is going to tell them more lies or something. I feel bad because Jeff is just getting better. I hope this doesn't set him back."

"Jeff still sounds sad and lethargic. He's kinda in zombie mode I think."

"When is the meeting?" I asked still racking my brain trying to figure out what her father was up to.

"It is this Friday evening at my parent's home. Do you think I should worry?" she asked with some concern. I could only imagine what she was feeling. She was the only protector, provider, and parent now. She had so much to handle and she was still dealing with the memories. At least I could help her with those. This new wrinkle had me worried.

"Well, I don't think it is anything to worry about until the meeting happens. Who knows, maybe he is taking them all to Hawaii and leaving you home as punishment."

We both laughed at the absurdity of the thought.

"Okay, I won't worry then."

"If you hear anything else, let me know immediately, will you? And keep the security alarm on and the doors locked." A foreboding feeling told me I needed to keep in close contact with Dani. I just didn't trust her father. He was very good at persuading anyone who would listen.

He had been able to keep his secret for years. Yes, he must be very good at it. He was up to something, I just knew it. Oh, to be a fly on the wall on Friday! I knew that wasn't going to happen so I just had to be content with being patient and waiting.

Nothing really happened for the next few days. I checked in with Dani to see how she was doing on supplies and to see if she had any bills that weren't paid that I could help with. She responded with kindness but insisted that Jeff would be home soon and he would take care of everything. I certainly hoped so but wasn't so sure. The kids were going stir crazy from being kept inside but after discussing it with her, she felt it was best that they didn't go anywhere for a while.

I almost didn't notice the arrival of Friday. I was busy with work and family activities. With children and grandchildren there always seems to be a birthday or soccer game or something to celebrate with them. We had just returned home from one such family gathering when my phone started vibrating.

"Hi, Dani, what's up?" I tried to sound cheerful and not tired like I felt.

"Jeff just called. They had their meeting tonight," she began.

"What did Jeff say?" I asked.

"He said that my father talked for a long time about me and how unstable I was and how I was off my medications. He told them he was afraid the children were in danger and that I was unstable and liable to hurt them." She paused fighting back tears and emotion. "That's not true, is it?" she asked in a way that sounded like deep emotional pain.

"No, Dani, you are not unstable and you are not a danger to your children," I replied to comfort her.

"Well, they are on their way here."

"What?" I asked with an intake of breath. "What do you mean they are on their way?"

"Everyone agreed that I was a danger and that I needed to go back home with my dad and live with him. He will take care of me and the kids and help me get over being crazy."

What she was saying was beyond belief. I had not seen this coming and felt completely blindsided by this turn of events! So, that was what it was all about. He was using Jeff's unstable condition to gain his support, along with the rest of the family, to force Dani to return to him and to the abuse. He couldn't have hoped to accomplish it without Jeff's support. Now it was clear how his lie to Jeff had started this snowball of events rolling. And it was working.

"So," she continued, "I am going back as soon as they come. I am sorry." Her voice choked and her tone had resignation in it.

"Dani?"

"What?" she answered.

"Do you want to go back to live with your dad? Do you know what will happen?" I needed desperately for her to see the absurdity of the situation and fast.

"No, but I have to."

"Why?" I asked.

"What do you mean?" she asked reaching out for some help, for some reason not to go.

"What do you think will happen to the children if they go to live in your father's house?" I asked hoping this would help her see what was happening.

"He will abuse them, too." she replied slowly as if she were considering the past with the present.

"Do you want that?" I asked.

"No."

"Then don't let it happen. If the whole city got together and decided you had to go back, you don't have to listen to them. Your first responsibility is to your children, to protect them. Remember the new rules?"

"Yes, I remember. So, what do I do? They are on their way." she said as if time had run out.

Quickly I assessed all the options. Did I have time to get over to her house? If I did, what could I do? I could try to reason with them but that would be like reasoning with the devil. They had family and Jeff on their side. I would be outmatched. There was no time to obtain an attorney. She couldn't just barricade herself in the house because Jeff had keys and knew the security codes. I was just as quickly running out of options. Then the Spirit quietly reminded me of something I had almost forgotten.

"Dani? Do you still have the backpacks in the back of the van?" I was praying that she had followed my instructions and hadn't removed them.

"Yes, why?" she asked.

"Grab the kids and leave the house immediately. Grab what medications or things you can get. Take one or two minutes tops, understand? Then get them into the van and leave. Understand? You must do it now."

"Okay. But where do I go?"

"When you are in the car and driving away we'll figure that out. Right now, hang up and leave."

The line went dead and my heart was stuck somewhere up in my throat. I just hoped that she could get out of the house and off before they showed up.

CHAPTER 18

Escaping Abuse

> *"Pain is temporary. It may last a minute, a day, or a year, but eventually it will subside and something else will take its place. If I quit, however it lasts forever."* –Lance Armstrong
> –From Dani's Diary

The moments had an agonizing way of dragging on. In my mind, I could see her heading out of the door only to be met by her father and other family members. I could see Jeff standing to the side not caring. I was kicking myself for not figuring that this would happen. If I had anticipated this we could have acted sooner. How could I have anticipated it? I struggled mentally.

I could see the logic in the plan. What her father was doing was trying to isolate her from all that she knew. By enlisting the vote of the family members and taking advantage of Jeff's condition, he had been able to manipulate both sides of the family into a consensus that Dani was indeed crazy and that they had every right to step in. So far it was working. I only hoped she could get out in time. Could this be checkmate? I prayed that it wouldn't be.

I tried to keep busy with work but I couldn't get the plight of Dani and her children out of my mind. A half hour had passed and I still hadn't heard from her and I had had enough. I grabbed my car keys and started for the door when my cell phone rang.

"Are you okay?" I asked anxiously.

"Yes," she replied in an amazingly calm voice, "we are safe."

"Did you have any problems?" I didn't want to keep shooting out questions but I was overwrought and was anxious for answers.

"We got into the car and headed down the street. I had the thought to take a different route than I usually do, so I did." She paused, indicating that she was proud of her choice. "Just as we were turning the corner I saw my dad's car turning down my street in the rearview mirror."

I nearly heaved a sigh of relief.

"So," she continued lightly, "I decided to drive carefully like you taught me, to make sure I wasn't being followed."

"But, where are you now?" I asked. I wondered if she was just driving around aimlessly with no thought of a place to go.

"I called a friend of mine," she continued as though she had not heard my question, "and told her we had a small emergency and asked if we could stay with her for a day or two. So, I parked the car in her garage and we are at her house."

I sat in amazement. Without any sign of panic and with no help from me, she had calmly made the decisions necessary to take care of her children and herself. She had escaped the trap laid by her father and had accomplished it with just seconds to spare. I couldn't help but imagine an angry and frustrated man going from room to room in the house only to find she and the kids had not obeyed the directive to stay there and wait for them.

"Dani, you did an amazing job. I am so proud of you. How long can you stay there?" I asked, thinking of our next move.

"We can stay a day or two at the most. I don't want to be any trouble for her and her family. She has been very kind."

In a wave of relief, I had almost let my guard down. She was safe, her children were safe, and so far, she had escaped abuse again. Then a thought came to me.

"Dani, does Jeff know about this place?" I asked.

"Yes, he does. Is that bad?"

"It just means that I need to work on another safe place they don't know about. At some point, they are going to question Jeff and he will probably think that you might have gone there. For right now, don't open the door for anyone. Okay?" I was hoping that this had not caused her friend's family to be in any danger.

"Okay," she replied, "we'll just hang out here."

Up to this point I had not considered any legal ramifications. My overriding concern was the safety of Dani and her children. I was quite sure that when her father had convinced the family that she was an unfit mother, he thought that was all he needed, hence no court document requiring Dani to surrender her children. Besides, that would involve Family Services.

Dani, on the other hand, was a grown woman capable of making her own decisions (which she had demonstrated today) even though she hadn't been allowed to most of her life. She had actually made this decision on her own after considering her resources. Jeff, on the other hand, had called her and had given her no options. I didn't even want to consider what would have happened by now if she hadn't called me.

Eventually they would try to expand the search to include any of Dani's friends and acquaintances. If that was the case then I had only a very narrow window of time to find another place of safety that they knew nothing about.

As clergy, I had been given a number of possible resources for such situations. I located the information for a confidential woman's shelter. I had no clue where they were located, as that was given out on an as-needed basis. This shelter was a non-profit group that accommodated women who were in immediate danger of violence during times when their lives might be threatened. I didn't know if Dani's situation would qualify. I started punching the numbers into the phone when I saw that I had an incoming call from Dani.

Hitting the reply key on my phone I asked, "Dani, are you okay?"

"Yes, silly, we are all fine," she replied.

"Well, how is your temporary home away from home?"

"It's okay. They are very kind and the kids are playing with their kids."

"I am glad. Thank them for me, will you?" I asked.

"I will," she replied. "I just thought I'd tell you I got a call from a concerned neighbor friend of mine."

"What did your neighbor say?" I asked.

"She said two men came to her house. They said they were with the police and were looking for me and wondering if they knew where I had gone because they were concerned for my safety."

"Then what happened?" I asked impatiently.

"She asked them for some identification. They didn't have any, they just turned around and went to the next house."

"Did she tell them anything else?" I asked.

"She didn't have anything to tell. She doesn't know what was going on. They just left. What do you think it means?" Obviously, Dani didn't know what to think of it.

"I am pretty sure they were not police. My guess is that they were your brothers or someone else your dad put up to this. You should be just fine where you are. Don't take any calls unless you can trust them. Understand?"

"I understand. And thank you."

"Why *thank you*?" I asked.

"We are safe. I can't imagine what would have happened if I had stayed."

"Me neither," I replied, "me neither."

Later that afternoon I finally reached the shelter by phone. It wasn't so much that they were the right choice but rather I needed to make sure that if Dani and her children went there it would be right for them.

The receptionist connected me to the director. I found that this was a secure facility allowing no entry to anyone unless they were screened. She told me how the facility had mostly women who had been beaten or abused in some way. This shelter allowed them a brief safe place from the violence to allow them to recover and get a hold on their lives again. They had a common area for the children, shared kitchen facilities, and private sleeping areas. Their mission, she told me, was to help and protect women and children from violence and abusive situations.

The bad news was that they were full for another 24 hours but then they would be able to accommodate Dani and her children. They could stay for only a few days.

Satisfied, I made arrangements for Dani and her children to arrive later the next day. This decision allowed me to buy some more badly needed time. I knew it would only be for a few days but I was confident that I could locate something more permanent within that time frame. There had to be someplace that she could go that they would not be able to find her or the children and they could be safe. I didn't know where, but I had faith in God that He would show me something.

I took some time to consider her situation and weigh all the possibilities. It was almost like a chess game; each side of those in Dani's life making moves, anticipating what the opponent's next move might be. I had not anticipated the phony police going door to door. Then it occurred to me that there was a police car that had often parked outside her house over the past several months. What the connection was I didn't know. Did her father have a friend in a police department somewhere? Were they now using police resources to track her down? Would they put a BOLO out on her vehicle? Her dad certainly could make the argument that she had maybe kidnapped the kids and they were in danger. These were variables for which I had no answers. What I did think I had in my favor was that they probably were under the misconception that Dani was acting on her own. They were thinking that with her limited knowledge, experience, and lack of contacts, she wouldn't be able to get very far. They knew she would be scared of the police and would be too scared to leave the city or travel any distance. They knew that it was only a matter of time and they would locate her.

The only plausible solution was to get Dani and her little family out of the situation and far away where no one would possibly think of looking for them. She just needed to disappear for a while. All of these thoughts presented themselves as I tried to consider our next moves. It appeared that we were keeping just one or two steps ahead of them. If that was all we could accomplish at a time, then it would have to do.

When evening came I called to see how they were and to make sure they were safe. I then presented my options to the Lord and asked for His guidance and then went to bed exhausted.

The following day went without incident. I called Dani around mid-morning and let her know I had made arrangements at the woman's shelter. She was real hesitant because she didn't know anyone there and it was unknown to her. After reassuring her that it was secure, safe, friendly and only temporary until I arranged something else, she relented. I arranged for a time to meet her and escort her to the shelter the next day.

I had received no phone calls either from Jeff or any family members. Either they were thinking that Dani was acting alone or they were afraid to call me. I just didn't know which one it was and nor did I care. The thought occurred to me that maybe I was just overreacting and that the emergency was just in my head. Something, though, told me that I wasn't overreacting.

It was mid-afternoon and only a couple of hours before escorting Dani to the shelter when I received a call on my phone.

"They were just here," she said with a touch of fear in her voice.

"Are you okay?" I asked.

"Yes," she replied, "we are just scared."

"What happened?"

"All of a sudden, there was a pounding on the door. I don't know if they could hear us from outside or not. But they pounded on the door and then the windows. We all huddled in the corner of the room. I tried to comfort the kids and keep them from crying."

"Are they still there?" I asked.

"I don't think so," she said. "We haven't heard anything for a while."

"Did you see who they were?" I asked.

"I didn't dare. We have just been huddled here."

"Are you ready to go to the shelter?" I asked.

Without any hesitation, she whispered into the phone, "Yes".

"I will be down as quick as I can," I announced and then ended the call.

I had anticipated they would locate places she might be, but I didn't anticipate it happening so soon. That must mean that her father felt he had only a little time before his control over the family would dissipate. He was trying to locate her as quickly as he could before anyone in his circle changed their mind.

The address she gave me was not hard to find. I drove by the house and looked for anybody that looked suspicious. I didn't know what I was going to do if I found one. Luckily, I didn't notice anything that appeared to be a possible threat. Satisfied, I called Dani. Within seconds the garage door opened, her van backed out, and she pulled up behind me. The garage door closed.

"Is everyone doing okay back there?" I asked into my phone. I heard children laughing and excited to be doing something else.

"We are fine. Is it far to the shelter?" she asked.

"No," I replied. "It's only about a 20-minute drive. Stay close and we will be there soon enough."

I pulled out watching as she began following my car. I led our two-car caravan out of the neighborhood toward the direction of the shelter. At any moment, I anticipated that one of their posse would see us and start tracking us. I knew they were coming back and I was determined not to be there when they did.

As we drove, I tried to avoid main roads, major intersections, and freeways. I took the least familiar routes, just in case they were somehow able to detect us. I didn't want to take any chances. I called her a couple of times along the way and could hear kids singing and laughing. At least they were having a good time.

A few miles from the shelter I pulled into a beautiful park that was not too well known except among the locals. I liked it because I could watch cars from both directions and watch anyone who pulled into the park. If there was anything suspicious, I would be able to see it and have time to react. For their safety, I had to be sure that nobody had followed us. I felt pretty certain that they would not bother her and the kids with me standing around being obvious or with other people in the park.

"Why did we stop here?" she asked after everyone got out of the van. The kids ran to the playground or rolled in the grass. They were very excited for the stop.

"The shelter won't be ready for a couple of hours," I replied. "I thought this was as good a place as any to stop for a while."

She smiled, looked at her children having fun, picked up the baby and said, "Thank you."

After the kids had worn themselves out, everyone piled back into the cars. There hadn't been any reason for concern. I started to relax a bit knowing that we weren't followed and this little family would be safe soon.

Within a few minutes we drove into a parking lot matching the address I had obtained from the director of the shelter. It looked like an office building and had no signs identifying who the building belonged to. I went in first to make sure we were at the right place and then beckoned them to follow. The director met us with a warm and caring greeting which put Dani immediately at ease. Satisfied they would be safe I headed back home.

With the dawning of a new day I knew that I had about seventy-two hours to find them another more permanent place. I needed a solution by Saturday and my mind was searching for possibilities. Because Dani's father might have a police officer friend, I had asked Dani to shut her phone off and only turn it on when she had to make a call. She was to call me every few hours to check in.

By the end of the first day, Dani was feeling very out of place at the shelter and was hoping to be in a new place much sooner. Evidently, she was the only woman in the shelter that didn't have a black eye, some stitches, or an injury. I asked her to be patient while I was looking.

I started to get concerned because Saturday was coming up quickly. If I was going to arrange something it had to be quick. The only plausible solution kept coming back to my mind. I felt that I needed to relocate her to someplace farther away, one where they would never even consider seeking her. It was the only way she would be truly safe for any length of time.

I made a few calls to 'test the waters' in surrounding states, but they all seemed too far away. Nothing seemed to be coming together, and then it occurred to me that my brother lived in a small town approximately a four-hour drive from my home. Since I hadn't spoken with him by phone for quite a while, I didn't know whether his situation would even allow for some long-term visitors. In any event, he may even know someone in his ward who he would trust that might provide a solution for Dani's family. I decided to call him.

After exchanging the usual pleasantries, I started to discuss a little bit of the situation.

"I was wondering if you had anybody in your ward or neighborhood who might be able to take in this little family for a while. It would mean a lot to them to feel safe and get them out of a bad situation."

"For how long?" came his reply.

"At this point I just don't know. One month, maybe two? It is possible that she might need to relocate permanently with her children. Right now, I am only concerned for the short term. What do you think?" I waited for his answer.

"We have a lot of really good people here. Any one of them would take this family in without hesitation. Interestingly enough, we have a huge room at the back of our home that was recently used by one of our kids. It is empty now with its own bathroom. I would need to speak to my wife first but I see no reason why your little family couldn't stay with us."

"That sounds great. I really appreciate that you would even consider it," I responded both surprised and relieved. "It is possible you could literally be a life saver. Call me back after you speak with her, will you?"

"How much time do we have before we can expect her if my wife is in agreement?" he asked.

"She is in a shelter right now. I was hoping she could come your way on Saturday. I hope that is not too quick for you."

"Give me a bit of time and I will call you right back."

Within an hour I heard back from my brother. They were excited and were already cleaning and getting the rooms ready. My hastily hatched plan was working, another indication of heavenly guidance. Now all I had to do was see if Dani would agree and since her phone was turned off, I had to wait for her to call me. I had a peaceful feeling that the Lord had provided another way to protect Dani and her children. More miracles.

Within a couple of hours, I would have the opportunity to see how Dani would react to this new plan. It would certainly change her life. She was now the unknown variable. Staying here and not leaving her home could be her decision. This area was all she had known. If that was her decision I wouldn't be able to stop her. Then again, she may just wish to stay with friends. On top of that, I was waiting for the other chess player in this drama to make his next move. What he didn't know is that I was still making my moves.

"How is everyone doing?" I asked quickly answering my phone.

"We are okay. We feel awkward here and it is hard. I think the other women wonder why I am here but we are surviving until the next step."

That was the door I was hoping she would open. I was hoping that the discomfort she was experiencing would be a catalyst for her to make the next decision.

"Well," I began, "how would you like to begin an adventure?"

There was a short pause before she responded. "What do you have in mind?"

"As you know, they are looking for you. If you drive the streets and go shopping or see your friends, there is a good chance they will find you. I may not be able to be there to protect you."

I paused briefly to let her take that in. It was obvious that it would only be a matter of time before someone saw her or bumped into her.

"For a long time, I have felt that the best solution is for you and the kids to go to a place further away where they would not even think of looking for you. You would be safe and the kids could play outside without you worrying so much about them. So, this is where the adventure comes in."

"What do you have in mind?" she repeated cautiously.

I mentioned the small community several hours away. I explained about my brother and his wife and how excited they were to meet her and the children. The room, the privacy, and the safety seemed to appeal to her. I assured her that they were safe and the children would have other kids to play with.

She thought about it for all of two seconds and said, "When do we leave?"

I knew that it would be unwise to send Dani and her children out on an adventure such as this without an escort. I may have been feeling a bit paranoid but not knowing how my 'chess opponent' was playing, I was determined to make sure that nothing interfered with the plan. To help ensure this, I contacted two of the men in my congregation and asked if they could take a special assignment to escort Dani to a place about half the distance to by brother's home. I decided on a meeting place at a gas station near the south end of town near the freeway onramp. They were to escort her and ensure her safety to the drop-off point and then my brother was to meet her there and take her the rest of the way. Even if either of these men mentioned where she went, they would only have knowledge as far as the drop-off point. From there she could have gone in any direction. There would be no trail to follow. Once my brother directed her to his home, she would be safe for the first time in days, maybe even years, and we could all relax.

On Saturday, I met Dani at the shelter. She was packed and not too unhappy about leaving. Even though the place had afforded safety, she never quite felt comfortable there. She followed me to the prearranged location where my two young volunteers were waiting. I made sure she had money for gas and food and then sent them on their way.

I didn't hear anything until evening. I received a text that they had made it to my brother's home without incident. The kids were again excited to have a yard to play in and a place to stay. Dani sent a message a bit later letting me know it was a bit awkward since she didn't know them but they were very nice and friendly. I knew this would be a whole new experience for her. She would make new friends and have new experiences all without the fear of her father or abuse. She would be able to walk outside without fear for the first time in months. She could go for walks, explore the local area, and realize a freedom that she had probably never known.

Just before retiring that evening I had set my phone down beside the bed when I heard it vibrate. I picked it up and it displayed the following text:

"I am laying here watching my precious children sleep. I love being a mommy more than anything."

I smiled and reached to put the phone down when it vibrated again. Another text. This one made it all worthwhile and brought tears to my eyes.

"It is wonderful to be free."

CHAPTER 19

Happily Ever After?

*When I despair, I remember that all through history
the ways of truth and love have always won.
There have been tyrants, and murderers,
and for a long time they can seem invincible,
but in the end they always fall. Think of it . . . always.*
—Mahatma Gandhi

It worked! To those in Dani's world it was as though she had disappeared into thin air. Dani and her children were nowhere to be found. That was just the way I had planned it, or at least the way God had shown me, to keep Dani safe.

They, whoever *they* were did not give up easily. I indicate *they* because I was now convinced that Dani's father and others were following and intimidating Dani. This was evident by the car that parked in view of her house for almost a week after she left. They obviously had no success spotting Dani or her van. They eventually gave up. The men pretending to be police officers continued to knock on doors in the neighborhood for a few days. Those who were contacted either didn't know who she was or had no idea where she was.

The plan worked only because her dad, and everyone else in her life, had no idea how much I was involved in helping Dani. Her father must have been extremely frustrated and angry to have his carefully-devised plan dissipate before his eyes. He must have figured that eventually she would have to turn up. When she wasn't spotted driving her car, getting the kids from school, or at the store, it must have added to his aggravation. Dani had always been under his control and it was quite certain she had never done anything like this before.

The big questions were: *Where was she? Where could she have gone?* Even Jeff had no clue where his family was. Since the arranged meeting at the house to take away all of Dani's rights, he had continued his downward spiral. Without medication, his bipolar condition careened him out of control until he finally reached the point where he realized he needed help. It was for this reason the location of his wife and children remained a secret. As Jeff sought help and his medications took affect, he realized how complicit he had been in almost turning his wife over to an abusive father. He was devastated to the point where he cut off all contact with Dani's parents and siblings. He was so lost without his family that he could not bear to stay at the house and stayed with his father for a time. When he did stop by, the house reminded him of a mausoleum. No laughter, no crying, only toys that never moved from their solitary place with no child to give them life.

At first Jeff was angry about his wife's disappearance. Without his medications, he had believed his father-in-law's claims that Dani had been unfaithful, was an unfit mother, and a danger to both herself and her children. However, as he walked through the quiet house, he realized how much he missed his family. He was suffocating with loneliness and grief. He started to sob uncontrollably, sank to his knees, and did something he hadn't done in a long time: He prayed!

Hours away, Dani sat in a comfortable home laughing with her children. For the first time in her life she felt safe. It didn't happen all at once, of course, but over time she began to trust my brother and his wife.

There is a saying that goes, *Time heals all wounds.* I don't know how true it is but in the case of Dani, I know that time away from the constant threat of abuse and pain gave her time to gain a different perspective and enjoy some healing.

It is important to note that Dani did not experience a total *Happily Ever After* with her relocation. She continued to struggle with a flood of returning memories, not to mention adjusting to a new life.

"Well, how is the adventure going?" I asked when she answered the phone during one of my follow-up calls.

"Not so well," she replied gloomily. "Can I come home now?"

"Why?" I asked. "Is something wrong? Aren't they treating you okay?"

"Oh, yes. They are very kind. They have provided a wonderful place for us to stay."

"Then I don't understand. Why are you not happy?"

"Well, the kids are really bored. They miss their friends. And it is so difficult staying in our part of the house all day." She made it sound as if they were supposed to stay in the house all day. This was not what I was expecting.

"Why don't you go out? Take the kids to a park, or go see some of the sights round about."

"We can do that?" she asked. "We can leave when we want?" She almost sounded relieved.

"Of course, you can use the house all you want and if you want to go outside or for a ride or to the store, you can do it. Did you think you had to stay hidden?"

"Well, I don't really know your brother and his wife very well. They are very nice. They include us in family prayer and they seem to laugh all the time. I just don't want to intrude."

"Dani, you and the kids are totally safe there. If you need to get out, you can take the kids and explore. My brother has opened his house up to you and the kids. You are safe there, okay?" I felt sad that she did not have the same vision of living there as I did.

"And Dani?" I asked.

"Yes," she replied.

"It is okay to trust them."

"Okay, thank you," she replied.

Dani settled in to her new life. The kids enrolled in school. Her new home was not like the larger private home she was used to but it was workable for the time being. Unfortunately, the memories did not stop coming. She still received them, lived through them, and had to deal with them as she had with all the others. Now her ability to bounce back was quicker. Without all the distractions, she was able to develop her faith in God and allow Him to carry her burdens.

After a while, Jeff contacted her by phone. Dani was really good about not telling him where she was. He was back on his medications and expressed how horrible he felt about what had happened. He enjoyed speaking with the kids as well. I received an email from Jeff which told how much he was missing his children.

"I feel so alone coming home and not seeing their beautiful faces, smiles, and receiving their hugs and kisses. I look in their rooms and miss the laughter and even the arguing. Their beds have been unslept in for so long, the toys have not been played with and enjoyed by them. I miss not being able to go out and just be with them.

I care so much for their safety and I am willing to give anything to protect them, even my life. I hope it does not come to that as I want to be with them more and more each day. I love talking to each of them and hearing the good and bad, success and failure, joy and sadness. I feel incomplete without being with my little family."

After a month or so, and feeling it was safe, Jeff was allowed to drive to her location and meet with his family in a public park. Dani felt that keeping him in the dark about where they were living was important for the time being. Jeff and Dani ate up this time together and renewed their relationship and trust. By this time Jeff had completely cut off his dad as well for his participation in helping to split up his family. Dani demonstrated one of her very unique qualities. She forgave Jeff totally and completely.

The change that was Dani took years to accomplish. From the emaciated little girl that was drugged, frightened, and extremely timid to the young woman who was mature and able to make decisions about protecting her children was a miraculous change. She was determined to face the aftermath of abuse in her life. No longer were there any days of being beat and tortured to believe that God doesn't exist. Now, every day is an opportunity for her to love and appreciate God and Jesus Christ for providing a way for her to deal with the memories of her past. Dani is truly a remarkable woman.

EPILOGUE

Helping Victims of Abuse

It has now been several years since the events in this book took place. Dani is doing amazingly well now considering all she has been through. She has grown from being almost completely dependent with no self-esteem to a confident and independent young woman. Instead of being racked by past experiences, she has learned how to allow God to carry the burden leaving her to live a more peaceful life.

Eventually Dani returned to her home with Jeff fully on board to be a faithful protector and provider as well as committed to stay on his medications. They work together, play together, and worship together. Jeff now understands the abuse that took place in his wife's life and is very protective of her and their children. Dani is very active in her children's lives. She volunteers at school, attends their activities, and helps them with homework. She still finds time to be compassionate to the neighbors around her. In almost every way, she has endeavored to put the past behind her.

After the botched attempt to kidnap her, Dani's father knew he had lost the control he had worked so hard to maintain over the years. Knowing that her silence could not be guaranteed, he suddenly and without notice, moved out of the state. No doubt he realized that it would be only a matter of time before he would be confronted with his past abusive behavior as well as any other unlawful activities he had been a part of. Not too long after that, her parents divorced. The cycle of threats, house surveillance, and cars following Dani dissipated.

There is no doubt in my mind that God's hand was through it all. He worked miracle after miracle. He knew the end from the beginning, despite my occasional doubts. He never failed either of us, He never faltered, and He never left us alone. He quietly worked the miracle that is now Dani, and what an amazing miracle she is!

Because the abuse happened to Dani over a twenty-year span, or more, the memories did not stop when she returned home. She continued to deal with the horrifying experiences that encompassed her youth and early married life. To assist you, the reader, to understand some of the additional abuses that Dani remembered through these years, I have included snippets of additional abuses that Dani remembered as a result of her unique healing process. Some of these would be exceedingly graphic if fully described and are only briefly mentioned here.

** Dani remembered she was pregnant several times during her youth. Most of the time her father or someone else performed a crude abortion.

** During her teenage years, she was sold to several men for as much as six months at a time. During the day, she described how she would stay bent over and locked in a cupboard for eight to ten hours. At night, she would be a bed partner for her 'owner'. She remembered her father talking about how much money he received for her sale, which was a lot.

** She would occasionally send me an obituary of some of the men who had abused her and were now dead. Her memory was exact as she would remember each one and how they had raped her. Among the clippings she sent me was a lawyer, a mechanic, and an owner of a well-known jewelry store.

** There was a commercial building tucked away in a residential neighborhood. She remembered the name on the sign. It was a place that no one would suspect that such evil was happening within. On Friday night about eleven or twelve until about six in the morning, the parking lot would fill up and for most of the night, cars would come and go. Inside, Dani and other girls were sold for sex. She remembers seeing a couple of police officers who appeared to be watching and would sometimes participate. They would get their sex for free and provide protection.

** One night, in the back of the building, Dani and another girl were forced to lay down. One of the men took out a revolver and inserted the barrel into the other girl's vagina. She did not like it and struggled causing the gun to fire. The bullet went through her insides and exited through her shoulder. Dani remembers watching this young girl die.

** For a time, she stayed at the house of a judge, who was an 'owner'. During the day, she was locked in a room. She remembers hearing the judge discuss with her father how young runaway girls would come before his bench and he would order them over to child services. After the session, he would change the paperwork and funnel the girls into the organization and abuse.

** She remembers waking up in a dumpster. As the light illuminated the interior, she found she was laying on top of arms, legs, torsos, and heads of young girls who had died or been killed, cut up, and disposed of. She remembers seeing a couple of heads with sightless eyes looking at her. We determined later that her father must have put her in there to teach her what would happen to her if she wasn't totally obedient.

** There was a commercial place that had an opening in the ground where a furnace burned constantly. She remembers that when the owners weren't there, that an employee would let her father and others in to dump body parts in the incinerator to get rid of the body parts.

** Dani became acquainted with one girl that was older than she was. She kept telling Dani that she was going to escape. Dani pleaded with her not to try, that it would be dangerous. But the girl told her she could not stand it anymore. She was caught escaping and hit over the head. Thinking she was dead, someone started cutting her up. They found out she was alive and didn't care and didn't stop. Dani watched her suffer until she died.

A Serious Problem

Dani's story is both true and eye opening. There are girls like Dani in every community. Nobody noticed the abuse that she experienced which spanned decades. How many other children have experienced similar abuse? There is really no way to tell.

Earlier in the book, I quoted Edmond Burke who said, "The only thing necessary for the triumph of evil is that good men do nothing." This is a true statement. If we had acted in spite of fear, then we might have been able to save a child from abuse.

During the years Dani was growing up, there were people who must have noticed the abuse. Doctors, teachers, church members, and neighbors should have seen something and either did not know how to react or were afraid to get involved. These are typical reactions. However, lack of understanding and fear of getting involved do not help or protect the abused. The key is to get involved at some level and do something!

Here are a couple of real life heroes who chose to act:

Texas Pizza Worker Takes Smoke Break and Saves Kidnapped Child – from KRIS TV

On July 9, 2015 a young lady, 26 years old, stepped outside a Papa Murphy's in Corpus Christie, TX to take a smoke break. She broke her routine and stepped out front to take her break. She watched a white car pull into the parking area. She had just received an Amber Alert and the car appeared to match the description. The alert was for a 7-year-old boy who had been abducted. A man with a young boy stepped from the car. The boy appeared to be scared. She second guessed herself a couple of times and said to herself that it could them. She waited for the man to enter a store and then she ran to the car to verify the license plate. It matched! After calling the police, the man was arrested and the boy was returned home. Courney Best, who received the Amber Alert and acted, is a hero.

Denver Father gets 5 years in Prison in "horrific" child abuse case - The Denver Post – December 30, 2014

A father of four boys was sentenced to 5 years in prison for keeping his sons in an apartment covered in human and cat feces. The boys, 2, 4, 5 and 6 years old could not speak or recognize their names. They didn't know how to eat a sandwich or know what an apple was. Since their rescue, the four boys went through a total of six surgeries. The police were notified after the mother took the youngest child to the hospital for treatment of a cut on his head. The hospital personnel who notified police are heroes.

3 Starving Children Rescued from a California Home of Abuse – Lee Baines - March 22, 2014

Three starving children, ages 8, 5, and 3 were rescued by police performing a welfare check after being notified that the children had missed some appointments. The sheriff indicated he had not seen anything like this in his 30 years and that the children looked as though they could have come out of a concentration camp. The little girl appeared to have taken the bulk of the abuse and was kept in a closet as well, shackled around her ankle as well as by a collar on her neck, to prevent her from obtaining food. The individuals who noticed that these children had missed their appointments and called authorities are heroes.

It doesn't take huge heroic acts, but it does take noticing what is going on around you and acting when something just doesn't look right. We need a lot more quiet heroes to rescue those children who cannot speak or act for themselves.

RESOURCES

Below are links that I found easily while doing a Google search by entering 'child abuse organizations in (enter your state)'. These are not an endorsement but a demonstration of how you can locate organizations in your area. These organizations are attempting to help and assist those who are abused. You should perform your own due diligence as to how reputable these organizations are. After you locate one, you can support it. Go to their website, review their mission statement. Many of these were started because the principles were either victims of abuse or had a family member abused. Find one or several; they could use your help both financially and as a volunteer. Just get involved. Another way to get involved is to become educated. There are several websites that will describe what to look for and what to do if you think someone is being abused.

Below are a few internet results of a recent search I conducted in the following states.

Arizona

    Child Help – a non-profit charity
    https://www.childhelp.org/

    Prevent Child Abuse in Arizona
    www.pcaaz.org/

Colorado

    Prevent Child Abuse Colorado – a non-profit charity
    www.preventchildabusecolorado.org/

Utah

    Citizens Against Physical and Sexual Abuse
    www.capsa.org/

Nevada / California

    Olive Crest
    https://www.olivecrest.org/

National Organizations

    National Council on Child Abuse and Family Violence
    https://www.nccafv.org/

National Children's Alliance

    www.nationalchildrensalliance.org/

Lastly, if you are reading this and you are in an abusive situation, there are numerous organizations that will help remove you out of any abusive situation. Abuse is wrong. You don't have to live in abuse. You may be worried about the consequences of trying to escape from abuse. Just like Dani, you can get out of abuse. You can live the life God has in store for you. Don't give up hope. God is always there.

REFERENCES

Davis, J. L. (n.d.). *Cutting and Self-Harm: Warning Signs and Treatment.* Retrieval date withheld, from http://www.webmd.com/mental-health/features/cutting-self-harm- signs-treatment#1

Faith Leaders Working with Victims of Domestic Violence and Their Abusers (Publication). (2004). Salt Lake City, UT: Utah Domestic Violence Council, Interfaith Leaders Committee.

Kennedy, J. (1962). May 17, 1961: Address by President Kennedy to the Canadian Parliament {Extracts}. In *Documents on Disarmament 1961*(Publication 5). Washington, DC: United States Arms Control and Disarmament Agency.

Millard, H. (Composer). Abide with Me; 'Tis Eventide in *Hymns of the Church of Jesus Christ of Latter-day Saints.* (1985). Salt Lake City: The Church of Jesus Christ of Latter-day Saints. (no. 165).

Olsen, K. (1992). My Father's Care. *New Era.* August 1, 1992.

Oz, F. (Director), Ziskin, L. (Producer), & Schulman, T. (Writer). (n.d.). *What about Bob?* [Video file].

Stephens, E. (1977). *Hymns*, Church of Jesus Christ of Latter-day Saints. (p. d143). Louisville, KY: American Printing House for the Blind.

Teller, E., & Shoolery, J. L. (2002). *Memoirs: a twentieth-century journey in science and politics.* Oxford: Perseus Press.

If you would be so kind,

please take a moment and leave an honest review on

Amazon.com